The Oasis

Born in Cambridgeshire in 1949, Phil Clarke left school 'essentially' at 14, was a factory electrician for 3-years, a scientific instrument technician for 6-years, then a full-time student for 4-years. After an incongruous year as a maths teacher, he spent a decade in the broadcast industry as a technician/engineer then operator before heading out around the USA (driving 16,000+ miles) then Australia and New Zealand for the best part of a year – since when he's ended up in Hastings UK where he was briefly a BT telephone operator. More recently he's driven around the EU a few times in a beaten-up old Jag, hostelling and camping, and otherwise cycles, walks (with the occasional sprint), sea-swims and generally idles about. Now and then, in dull moments and for several decades, he's followed various literature, philosophy, psychology, and other underhand activities, especially from 'alternative' & independent sources - and from which, occasionally, he might cook-up a little treatise or essay (as here) from what he makes of it all. Hence, these articles – sifted for their relevance to making our lives more enjoyable and fulfilling - are an amalgam of the objective and subjective: facts that are frequently self-evident, and what's from personal experience: see also: zoneidle.co.uk

BY THE SAME AUTHOR

Tales of the Abnormal
Essays and Sketches
The First 40 Years (memoir)
The Coming Nuclear War
Great Writers

Phil Clarke

THE OASIS

And how to navigate it

A personal approach

This is an uncorrected early edition. If you've enjoyed reading it, have any criticisms or comments you feel like making, then please visit the book's Amazon page and make them there.

Many Thanks...

Copyright © Philip Clarke 2023

The right of Philip Clarke to be identified as the author of this work has been asserted by him in accordance with the Copyright, Designs and Patents act 1988.

ISBN: 9798864666999

for Stew

Across the Fields

Across the sky, the clouds move,
Across the fields, the wind,
Across the fields the lost child
Of my mother wanders.

Across the street, leaves blow,
Across the trees, birds cry –
Across the mountains, far away,
My home must be.

Hermann Hesse

6

CONTENTS

Note		9
1 -	Other books	11
2 -	Intro	13
3 -	The Oasis	15
4 -	The Background	17
5 -	The Skill-Master	19
6 -	Mind for Itself – escape	25
7 -	The Story of Hari	30
8 -	You Can't Be Serious?	36
9 -	A Chance Episode - Thoughts of a Sage	39
10 -	Studs Terkel	43
11 -	Zen	49
12 -	Going Wild	59
13 -	Change Your Mind	64
14 -	Consciousness & Conscience	69
15 -	Ronnie Laing	74
16 -	Sleep	84
17 -	Hell Is Other People	91
18 -	Conclusion - the final whole	96
Appendix - 'Trees'		98

Note

THIS BOOK, like any book, addresses the intellect. This means it can have minimal effect on the subconscious. The subconscious is only influenced by real experience, and by frequent practice at whatever we aim to master. I can read and re-read the most articulate books on the planet about how to play a violin, but none of it will mean I can pick-up a violin and play. Only practice will make that possible even if I read nothing. My hope is that this book will nudge and motivate readers to practice what they judge will work for them so they experience more of what their subconscious needs to ultimately transform crucial aspects of it from negative to positive, from feeling dominated by some inner demon to a new freedom of mind.

So the aim is to provide a set of ideas and suggestions that can be adopted and built on to make life more tranquil, enjoyable and fulfilling. One approach is through observing techniques that have worked for millennia, but with user-friendly variations such as chapter-6 with my version of mediation. In fact, if you prefer to dive straight in then skip this page for now and go there instead - but do return later.

Some sections of this book may seem irrelevant, simplistic, or even soppy. But one person's sop is another person's solace; and a bit of clever sop, like good poetry, can sometimes have a profound effect, especially if contemplated awhile.

Alas, though, for some people life is experienced largely as torturous and filled with nightmares. It's all about what's in your head and the forces there that spar for precedence. Even so, to take a few minutes now and then (or even days....) reflecting on little verses like the last lines from Lewis Carol's

'*Alice Through the Looking Glass*' can in some circumstances prove very uplifting:

In a wonderland we lie,
Dreaming as the days go by,
Dreaming as the summers die,

Ever drifting down the stream,
Lingering in the golden gleam,
Life, what is it, but a dream?

Reading and pondering the work of some great poets, and some not so great, can prove a worthwhile project for many people.

1

Other Books

OVER THE YEARS I've glanced into several books on how to manage, change, improve... Your Life! These have been around since the 1930s - and probably, in their various forms, from well before that. But in recent times their number has positively exploded. They are everywhere nowadays, new and second-hand — often newly second-hand (presumably, they attract a purchase and then disappoint — for reasons I examine shortly). Whatever their effectiveness, though, they fall essentially into two distinct groups:

First, there are those designed for workaholics. These attempt to inspire the reader to re-examine their life with the aim of challenging the constant effort and toil that enslaves them. The reader is encouraged to instead awaken to the real values of existence - like to just enjoy being alive. The intension here is to help readers abandon futile hopes of future material wealth, fame or some other crazy idea and instead recognise and reach out for an achievable sustained contentment in the here and now. I suppose this, in a capitalist society, could be seen as subversive.

The second kind are for idlers. These attempt to persuade the reader to shove their nose ever more securely to the grindstone. They do this by concentrating on efficiency, maximising resources, especially time and energy, and promoting the *Will to Achieve*. The emphasis here is on motivation, on striving to fulfil one's potential in a competitive world. In complete opposition to the first, this type of 'self-help' could be seen as an attempt to endorse, rather than subvert, capitalist principles.

There are aspects where these two types of book intersect, notably on motivation: to focus on whether you seek to avoid effort and enjoy life for itself, or to engage in effort to achieve great wealth, high status or some other lofty aim.

Some books, inevitably, will be more successful than others in nudging their readers towards action (or inaction). But I'm sceptical of how effective *any* of them can be in actually evoking change in the lives of more than a few percent, if that. And probably those few will mostly comprise people already well focussed on similar intentions.

But assuming a book *is* effective, then what might its effect be? If those for whom the book is primarily intended *are* persuaded by its suggestions, then some readers might achieve a level of moderation in their lives. I recoil, though, at the thought of a workaholic taking up the second kind. The result might be precisely the sort of psychopaths that become senior politicians, CEOs of big corporations or master criminals etc: in other words, the most greedy, ruthless, primitive and destructive face of humanity possible. I can't imagine a mere book achieving such a result; besides which, psychopaths are not made from reading books. On the other hand, if an idler takes up the first kind, then something quite different might be achieved, perhaps akin to what Studs Terkel unearthed: see chapter-10.

2

Intro

SO IN CONTRAST to the usual self-help books, this book takes a different approach. It forms my response to a request from my friend X for something quite unlike the standard coffee-table tomes that may prove a nice read but invariably fail in their asserted objective.

This, on the other hand, is for anyone who truly aims to distance themselves from the causes and triggers of trauma and stress, and to instead enjoy the mental freedom that serenity brings. Not that this book contains any kind of expert treatise on serenity - that's up to you, as ever - but it does introduce several angles that, I believe, could prove to work more effectively than most other approaches. Hopefully, it's also easier to read, as well as more engaging and motivating than the usual expositions.

Various kinds of medication, aside from 'accepted' anti-depressants, have been shown to work admirably in reducing recurring trauma even to zero. But so also have some hallucinogenic medications; for instance, psilocybin 'magic-mushrooms', lsd and maybe even cannabis can work to an extent. For anyone who has access to these through reliable sources and can take them under competent supervision, I'd say do so: Life is an ongoing series of experiments, but either way follow this book and pick what you think could help, especially if meds are not available.

As to 'accepted' meds, it was recently announced by a Swedish research outfit that trials had concluded that for most people suffering depression, frequent moderate exercise has the same beneficial and lasting effects as a course of antidepressants.

We are all individuals with different back-stories and different kinds of needs, so we first have to find what we think will work best for us – which might well be a bit of everything? I include many quotes in this book, not least from one of my favourite natural philosophers: Henry Miller, whose most poignant quote of all, I think, is:

> *'Life, as it is called, is for most of us one long postponement.'*

When I first read that, it almost made me shudder. The obvious implication is too negative to contemplate when life is so short:

> *"Remember, dear friends, now and then, just for a moment, how short life is."*
>
> Hermann Hesse

3

The Oasis

IMAGINE YOU'RE MOVING along an infinite line that represents time. You exist now on that line at a point called 'the present'. Looking back along the line, you can go trillons of years, and despite chance, entropy, chaos and everything else that's happened in the universe, logically-speaking your existence was always inevitable: because you're here, the stage was always set for you to exist.

Imagine another infinite line that crosses your personal timeline. This represents space, so you have a gigantic X of infinite time crossing infinite space. The point where the lines cross is where you are NOW in space: on planet Earth.

Imagine it: all through time you've been in the blackest of nights crossing a desert of nothingness. Vast numbers of every possible creature flow there, each on their unique personal timelines, but *except for a minuscule few* they're ghosts, potential beings doomed to eternal non-being and forever oblivious of existence and of themselves.

You are one of the minuscule few. Your timeline was destined for you to enter the oasis. You had no choice of whether, when or where you entered. Some entrances are booby-trapped and send the new entrant straight back to the desert. And once back, there's no return - you continue on your timeline in eternal non-being. Some people believe we do return; this seems unlikely to me - though who am I to say?

Everyone reading this will be established in the oasis: think of it as an elongated strip of many kilometres, floating free in that infinite desert of nothingness – a solitary island in outer-space. Some of us enter at a point of turmoil and desolation, others into tranquillity and abundance, with all variations between.

Yet as we acclimatise and begin to cross the oasis, we never know quite where we are. We can choose to skirt the edge like mountaineers and racing drivers, or head for what seems safest where fountains spring and palm-trees grow. But at any moment our next step could propel us back to the desert. Our route ahead, towards what we might picture as some kind of paradise, will be easy and short for some, gruelling and tough for others. We learn from experience how best to navigate through, how to make the most of our fleeting brush with consciousness, which we can only experience in the oasis and lose the instant we leave.

Our predicament brings to my mind the genie trapped in his bottle for untold aeons until by lucky fluke the stopper is removed and he's set free at last – then years later he's finally tricked back into the bottle where he then remains for all eternity.

4

The Background

FIRST TO SAY: like some aspects of life, not all sections of this book will be relevant to everyone. Regard it like a buffet: some items will be tasty and just what you're looking for, while others might seem best avoided - at least, placed aside, as it were. Second: most of what I've discovered that's appropriate to the issues I address here is from other books and writers, both ancient and modern, as well as experience from within myself and interactions with people I've known.

I recognise too that my own background has been relatively uneventful and benign. At least, I'm not aware of my past returning to haunt me. I guess I belong to the lucky few – which I admit hardly qualifies me to write a book like this. But one observation from personal experience strikes me as profoundly significant in how past events can have a lasting impact.

When I was about 5-years old, walking slowly in a quiet street with my parents, nibbling a cheese biscuit that had a particular flavour, we were startled by a sudden loud roar and ringing bell. I turned to see a fire engine rapidly approaching. In those days - the 1950s – fire engines carried a huge bell above the cab. As the engine rushed past, its bell clanging wildly, I went rigid for a few seconds gripped by something akin to fear. The sense of high drama left me tense and alarmed for several minutes, I remember – someone's house was on fire and people were burning. For years afterwards, maybe a decade, whenever I tasted one of those kinds of biscuit, I felt first a twinge of alarm – then a second or two later memory of the fire engine would loom in my head.

I believe our lives are full of associations like this, mostly trivial and innocuous, but for some unlucky folk they can be devastating and last much longer than a mere decade. Traumatic events from our early years may be heavily repressed and impossible to recall. But our reactions to trauma from an associated trigger (ie, the cheese biscuit) will brings back the sensation aroused at the time (ie, fear). I guess this is the essence of Post Traumatic Stress Disorder (PTSD).

I'm no psychiatrist nor psychologist, though I've read a bit here and there on related issues, notably from Ronnie Laing and Carl Jung. Hence, as I say: this booklet is mostly what I've deduced from a range of sources that might – just might – help someone who finds the usual 'self-help' books boring or ineffective, as they frequently seem to me when I've dipped into them.

5

The Skill-Master

THE OLD ADAGE that you can't change other people, and people can only change themselves is probably true. And since we are where we are now at this moment, moving forward in time, carrying only what our past has provided - good, bad, indifferent, whatever - then it's up to us to begin any change we wish to make in ourselves. True, other people can make this easy or difficult. As Sartre famously observed: *"Hell is other people"* – but failed to add: *"So is heaven."*. It is up to us to take charge here – if we possibly can...

Remember also, like my cheese biscuit, most childhood associations fade, at least a little, as we age and mellow. Some, alas, do remain prominent, especially the more traumatic - and it's this above all that I'm focused on in this book.

You may fit one of the 5 basic types of people – or is it 9, or even 13? But each of us has a unique personality and set of attributes. This means what works for one won't necessarily work for another. Do we really need to find what gave rise to a trauma in order to exorcise it or its trigger, or do we just need to avoid the triggers – or should we learn to master our feelings or responses when a trigger occurs?

Psychology may have clear answers to questions like these, but I imagine it depends more on the individual, how strongly a trauma was felt, how long it continued, and how the victim responded at the time.

Henry Miller eloquently addresses one kind of crisis that can trap or overwhelm, for instance: *"The real escapists are they who adapt themselves to a world they do not subscribe to."* My response to which is to ask: Is there *anyone* who subscribes to everything in this world? Miller continues:

> *"...only when I got to France, where I came to grips with myself, that I realized that I alone was responsible for all the misfortunes which had befallen me. The day that truth dawned on me – and it came like a flash – the burden of guilt and suffering fell away. What a tremendous relief it was to cease blaming society, or my parents, or my country. "Guilty, Your Honor! Guilty, Your Majesty! Guilty on all points!" I could exclaim. And feel good about it....*
>
> *"Of course I have suffered since, many times, and undoubtedly will continue to do so ... but in a different way. I am now like those alcoholics who, after years of abstinence, finally learn how to take a drink without fear of becoming drunk. I mean that I have made my peace with suffering. Suffering belongs, just as much as laughter, joy, treachery or what have you. When one perceives its function, its value, its usefulness, one no longer dreads it, this endless suffering which all the world is so eager to dodge. When it is regarded in the light of understanding it becomes something else. I called this process of transmutation my "rosy crucifixion." Lawrence Durrell, who was then visiting me (at Villa Seurat), expressed it in another way; he dubbed me 'as of henceforth'* The Happy Rock.*"*

Miller comes to terms with what he calls suffering, accepts it as a necessary part of life, so practices and teaches himself - maybe not to relish it - but to embrace it. Soon he ceases to experience it as suffering; he's learned to master it. Miller seems to have taken a similar approach as Colin Wilson in the following description of how he learned to master writing. And the same technique can be applied to any act or process, whatever you choose to engage in and wish to become proficient, even expert at - like finding tranquillity of mind:

> "As a writer, I am aware of the "feedback" process. My right brain produces the intuitions, my left has the task of turning them into words. When I was a beginner, I did it so clumsily that I usually killed the intuitions, and when I read it later, the words seemed dead and empty. Then I got better at it, until the left could catch the intuitions like a good fielder. Sometimes it did it so well that the right would get enthusiastic to see itself so well expressed; and then the left would be spurred to still greater efforts by the approval of the right and the whole process would build up until I felt positively 'inspired'."

That kind of feedback is one explanation for how practice can work. It's slow too, so one has to be fairly keen or attracted to the task, the 'art' – and at first not be too concerned about quality or achieving very much. This applies to any creative process: playing a musical instrument, learning another language, painting, sculpting, attaining contentment... achieving a level of freedom from associations and triggers.... anything your brain can be trained to mould to, and to master.

> ....when we learn to do something "automatically", says Wilson, it is transferred to the subconscious; and depending upon how much effort it has cost us to learn, it carries with it a label which says "important" or "unimportant". So when we perform a learned activity the subconscious energy evoked corresponds to its importance - ie, the degree of effort required to learn it.

So if you want to be a writer you start the slow process of creating inarticulate, stilted sentences that lack 'flow', then suddenly, after months of effort to no avail so it seems, and just when you think you'll never get it: *voila* – you notice for the first time some kind of coherence and natural rhythm that was previously so elusive. The skill has started to become established in the subconscious and is beginning to take-on an 'automatic' quality, so you don't have to think about it - the skill is embedding, in the same way that you don't have to think about walking as you did when a toddler. This recognition spurs you on, like the toddler next trying to run, or a pianist for the first time making the piano 'sing' little melodies without conscious focus on their fingers.

So you move onto the next stage, developing the skill on and on. The younger you start the greater the benefit. Practice shapes the mind and the shape sticks more firmly when young. If only I'd realised this as a youth!

On the first page of his most famous 'autobiographical' book '*The Tropic of Cancer*' (1934) written in Paris, Miller writes:

> "I have no money, no resources, no hopes. I am the happiest man alive."

A few pages on, after writing: '*When I say "health" I mean optimism.*'

> One day Carl wants to blow his brains out because he can't stand this lousy hole of a Europe any more; the next day he talks of going to Arizona "where they look you square in the eye."
> "Do it!" I say. "Do one thing or the other, you bastard, but don't try to cloud my healthy eye with your melancholy breath!"
> But that's just it! In Europe one gets used to doing nothing. You sit on your ass and whine all day. You get contaminated. You rot.
> Fundamentally Carl is a snob, an aristocratic little prick who lives in a dementia praecox kingdom all his own. "I hate Paris!" he whines. "All these stupid people playing cards all day ... look at them! And the writing! What's the use of putting words together? I can be a writer without writing, can't I? What does it prove if I write a book? What do we want with books anyway? There are too many books already. . . ."
> My eye, but I've been all over that ground - years and years ago. I've lived out my melancholy youth. I don't give

a fuck any more what's behind me, or what's ahead of me. I'm healthy. Incurably healthy. No sorrows, no regrets. No past, no future. The present is enough for me. Day by day. Today! Le bel aujourd'hui! *[The beautiful today]*

And I think: If only I could face each day like Miller - and not Carl.

The truth is that we're content to put great effort over a long period into teaching our right-brain to master some artistic skill, like as I say: writing or playing a musical instrument well, but how many of us would dedicate half-an-hour or so a day to some aspect of training our mind to become tranquil. That's to say: master itself, take charge, to become – at least briefly – our normally invisible REAL SELF that sits in our head above everything, watching what's going on in our mind, observing, detached from the anger, the sadness, the torment?

Our REAL SELF is the real us, what we were born with, and remains as it was before our minds (not to be confused with this REAL SELF) became corrupted, indoctrinated, twisted and battered about by the world around us. Zen describes how we can re-connect with our REAL SELF. See Chapter 11.

When I began writing, my efforts were disappointing at first; likewise if I'd tried learning to play a violin. I thought: if I can't achieve coherence and flow soon, then there isn't much hope. But I was determined, so persevered. But imagine, tired of fruitless effort, just when my skills were about to flip into the first level of coherence, I'd given up. Then I'd never have written anything. But I didn't give up, and with several more disheartening months of little progress, suddenly I noticed another crucial encouraging leap of coherence.

Whatever you wish to master: if you're determined, you'll persevere. Eventually, some will sink into your subconscious, and a small glimmer will be forthcoming. When that happens, it spurs you on; now you're getting somewhere. Next day the advance might fade a little, but you keep going because of that glimmer.... then suddenly, after weeks of practice, completely unexpected, a leap - the mastering is working, the effort is paying-off - before long, a further leap. The writing grips, the piano 'sings', the contentment – freedom from (or decrease in) despair, anxiety - if only briefly at first - is profound like a proverbial weight off your shoulders.

This, I imagine, is precisely what happens when someone meditates, not necessarily by sitting still with their eyes closed in a quiet room - for some reason that doesn't appeal to me at all, nor I believe to many people, but meditation as I describe in the following key section.

6

Mind for Itself

READ AND THEN TRY THIS:

There are many ways of achieving inner tranquillity and the sense of contentment that comes with it. The aim is to still the mind, which is usually preoccupied with worldly activities like reflecting on the past or projecting on the future. Hence the old adage for inner peacefulness: 'Living in the NOW'

The assumption is that NOW you are sitting comfortably at home in a quiet room, on a bench-seat in a park with birds singing and distant traffic sounds, or on a remote beach with the waves lapping or even crashing, gulls crying, wind blowing... or perhaps you're not sitting, but are in a busy street with all the sounds and bustle one associates with such places.... Crucially, though, you're focus is in the NOW... fully conscious of the present - even if powerful thoughts intrude and swirl stubbornly around in your mind, you focus on your senses: touch, sight, sound, taste, smell.

You are NOW free to feel the ground against your feet, the air on your face, the clothes on your skin – feel the input from your senses... one at a time, gradually relax muscle tensions: feet, then legs, body, shoulders, neck. Smell the air. If you're sitting, you can close your eyes and let the sounds around you float by while you listen over them and beyond for more distant sounds, then past those too until you're focused on the great far-off backdrop of silence.

Any thoughts in your mind, regardless of subject or cause, deflect your attention from them as if you're dodging locusts flying towards you. As thoughts revolve or new ones enter, steer your focus around them, letting them fade unfed by any kind of attention. If you can achieve that, if only for a few seconds, you are beginning to master your mind, you are beginning to MEDITATE.

Even if you're walking, looking at things as they pass by, keeping your focus in the NOW means you're riding on a crest of no-time, resting the mind. Notice consciously whatever enters your senses from touch and sight as they change, as sounds pass, constantly letting their memory go, to be replaced by a new NOW, so the NOWs merge to become that single crest of no-time. This is a kind of shallow meditation that's almost as restful as the deeper meditation when sitting quietly with eyes closed.

When I've meditated in a quiet room the quietest sound can be as intrusive as a dumper-truck if I'm meditating on a bench-seat near a busy building site. But by listening BEYOND the sounds I dismiss them, so can meditate virtually anywhere. Some people prefer a noisy background, so full of sound that it's impossible to latch onto any, making it easier to search beyond. Others prefer a quiet place, a church, a cemetery, a park or a beach.

In spite of trying to meditate and still the mind, most of the time I fail to achieve that stillness. Yet, as I say, even a few seconds of calm can make it all worthwhile, in fact a great achievement, with significant benefits. If you have negative thoughts that you believe need several hours to elapse in order to leave behind, then a few minutes of meditation can have the same effect – separating you in time – so you feel distanced and refreshed.

It's the psychological equivalent of a couple of minutes standing on one of those vibration machines at large exhibitions that rejuvenate one physically as if you've just arrived, when in fact you've already spent hours wandering around. All the aches and pains that were wearing you down – ie, all the worries and stresses that were dragging you into despair loading you with stress – are pushed into the distance in just a few minutes, reduced or even eliminated altogether.

The truth is, I rarely bother to meditate, as if to do so involves effort and that to remain fully aware of myself and my surroundings is a priority. By saying I rarely meditate, though, is not entirely correct, because what I mean is: I rarely do it deliberately. Rather, it's incidental as I wander through woodland, across fields and hills, into glens and lose myself among a maze of little paths... instead of ruminating I focus on the NOW: where I am, how it feels. This is easy when alone. But one can be anywhere, doing anything...

For a novice all this might seem astonishing or even weird – you only have to try it to see that it works. Watch that you don't build negative thoughts again by focusing on them after you've stopped meditating – by avoiding them you can remain refreshed. But why stop meditating, when you can change to a less deep version while you get on with other activities – making sure to focus on that activity while steering around reflections/anticipations that are not relevant to what you're doing.

I think we all spend our lives constantly moving through levels of meditation. It's as if there's a line at one end of which is Zero where the most disturbed/frenzied reflective/ruminating planning/anticipating brain activity is going on – ie, the lowest possible meditative condition – while at the other end is the deepest most tranquil meditation possible, such as perhaps Krishnamurti or Marharishi practiced.

All the time we are somewhere on that line between a mind in turmoil and a mind at peace. Most of us, I guess, move around near the centre. But if we give ourselves a few minutes near the peaceful end, we'll stick there a bit after we stop before slowly sliding back to almost where we were. If we do it often, every time the slide-back will be slower and less. So we become more composed, more contented and more responsive.

Our worries fade, maybe not altogether, but fade is a start. Our health improves, and our outlook too. NOW our brains can work on what they're most useful for – whatever we intend – instead of wasting emotional energy churning over all kinds of pointless, useless, irritating babble to no avail, babble that could be causing stress and unhappiness, like a niggling demon constantly pestering and stopping us operating effectively and contentedly.

So try it – but don't try too hard – as with life in general, these things are best approached light-heartedly. It can be hard to completely dismiss thoughts, as it can be hard to relax the body sometimes, so don't be concerned, just do what you can - eventually you'll get it. Big thoughts, from a bereavement, say, may be impossible to place aside and out of 'sight', but to give yourself distance is all, just to allow your mind a little space, a little rest.

There's loads of techniques: focussing on objects, mantras or real sounds. For me, none are especially effective. I merely sit, relax, rest attention on my senses – one after another – then listen through the sounds around me until I'm merging with that great peaceful void beyond everything. Once a few seconds of stillness has been achieved, I can return to normal, open my eyes refreshed, and get on with whatever I'm doing – or not doing – feeling more composed, more contented and at one with myself and the world as it is (warts an' all, as they say), but still watching-out to deflect unwanted intrusive thoughts, and being in the NOW.

Try to keep in mind – blank as one might wish one's mind to be, though it's hard, almost impossible to achieve - keep in mind that you can practice the above most of the time, and that the more you practice the easier it gets and the more effective the benefits.

When walking along the road practice Ouspensky's 'lamppost-trick'. What could be simpler: Just remember 'lamppost' so when you spot one you're reminded to hoist your mind into the NOW. Or 'tree' or anything. Be present where you are. Feel the pressure on you feet, the air on your face, observe the trees, cars, buildings, fields that you can see, smell and listen... focus on what your senses are detecting. Steer around thoughts so if they won't disappear, then at least they're shoved aside as secondary to the NOW. And the more you do that the easier it gets, the quieter the thoughts will become, and the closer you'll be to having a restful mind and contentment.

7

The Story of Hari

EVEN AT 19 YEARS OLD, Hari still nurtured hopes of stumbling on some fabulous path that would lead him to a future of happiness and fulfilment. For several years after leaving home he dreamt of nothing else, neglecting both himself and any thought of a conventional career. When his hopes came to nothing, he finally rejected everything and entered a turbulent unsettled period. At first destitute, wandering the streets by day, he soon found himself working as night cleaner in an office block. After being sacked for falling asleep in a broom cupboard, he took a job as a tanner in a shoe factory. By then he was able to afford a bed-sit, but he dreaded every minute in the tannery: the fumes, the wet, the continual standing. At his next job he ran errands for a debt collection agency, mainly delivering final demands. Frequently chased off and threatened by angry debtors, he soon threw that in too. Then he got work in a sprawling market lugging boxes all day, and in the evening cleaning up. When his back nearly gave out he changed again; and several times more he moved jobs, as well as dwellings, each no more agreeable than the last.

Now, as a kitchen porter for a large hotel, Hari lived in a box-room in the hotel attic where most of the junior staff were accommodated. The head chef, who'd had his eye out for a dogsbody, found Hari in the yard one day picking through the dustbins for scraps of food, and had – so Hari at first assumed - taken pity on him. But, as usual, exploitation set in, and Hari began to contemplate another change.

But then an important guest arrived, and rumours quickly circulated that it was Madam Rashdi, a famous spiritual sage from the East. Hari learned of this while washing a whole sack of potatoes in the out-house behind the big kitchen. One of the chef's assistants had been sent to warn him to keep hidden since he was the only one not required to look clean and smart.

The guest had demanded special food, declared the chef's assistant haughtily. She insisted on inspecting the kitchens, he said, and had appointed him, yes him, together with one of her entourage, to supervise the preparation of their meals. She was very particular, he told Hari, and the head chef would not tolerate Hari's presence in the kitchen in his dirty ragged condition.

Hari was not offended. He was used to his situation and resolved to do as was suggested without question. In any event, he preferred his position of no responsibility. Above all, though, he despised petty hierarchies and wanted no part in them; to him they reeked of subservience, ritual and duty, and of absurd rules that evoked unpleasant memories of school.

But completely unexpectedly, the important guest suddenly came waltzing through the kitchen and out into the yard. The head chef and manager scuttled behind her in a fluster, calling her back. But in spite of her graceful manner, she was too quick for them, and she put her head into the outhouse where Hari sat cleaning potatoes and wondering what the commotion was outside.

'What's this?' she exclaimed in a refined Eastern accent, 'Come outside into the light.'

As she backed away, the manager and chef moved quickly to one side, imploring her once more to return to the hotel proper. With his hands dripping with muddy water, Hari reluctantly followed her out and stood before them looking unkempt and neglected. And there they stood: the enchanting woman guest, the manager, the chef's assistant, and the chef -

who, with agitation and an expression of shame mingled with distaste, scrutinised the dank, grubby yard.

Beside the woman the others appeared dull and even somehow extraneous. Unlike them she radiated warmth and charm. She wore a long puffy pink dress with rippling furbelows covered in silver glitter, while her blond hair flowed onto her shoulders, and was adorned with several huge bows of pink silk. Hari detected the scent of jasmine. He had never before seen such a beautiful face on a woman who he judged was well into her fifties.

After studying Hari for a moment, she turned to the manager, who had never seen Hari before in his life, and said, 'This is the first person I have met since arriving in this town whose bearing exudes both humility and dignity. If he has no objection I would like him to be my first subject.'

'But I have many staff, madam, who are far more suitable.' pleaded the manager, 'This lad is untrained, off the street, as it were. His integrity is unknown.'

'That is precisely the ideal subject.' said Madam Rashdi, calmly waving the manager aside, and staring contentedly at Hari, 'Besides, it is quite clear from his face, so open yet so knowing... and indeed his very posture, so accepting yet so authentic... that his suitability is unquestionable.'

'But Madam...' implored the manager, glancing with revulsion at Hari. 'I really cannot accept responsibility for any complications that may arise.'

'That's settled then,' she replied, 'Hold me responsible.' Then, addressing Hari, said pleasantly, 'And what's your name?'

'Hari.' He said.

'Will you consent to be my first subject here?'

'What will I have to do?' asked Hari.

The manager and the chef fidgeted impatiently, shaking their heads and wringing their hands.

'To begin with, meditate.' said Madam Rashdi, 'For you it will be very simple. Then we shall see.'

Hari stared back, perplexed. But as he watched her, Hari became mesmerised and his mind filled with reminiscences of his former dreams. To the others standing there, it was Madam Rashdi's smile that won his consent. And as she turned and he followed her into the kitchen, the chef clicked his fingers at his assistant and signalled for him to attend to the potatoes. The assistant responded with an expression of horror, then lowered his head and trundled towards the outhouse.

Keeping close to Madam Rashdi, Hari entered the great foyer with it's chandeliers and plush carpet dotted with enormous pot plants. Normally Hari would have gazed around in wonder and curiously at all this but his eyes were fogged by Madam Rashdi's curious spell. She swept past the dining room and into a private lounge where, as soon as Hari was in, a young woman in Eastern dress closed the door and followed them into the room.

Madam Rashdi took a cloth from a little box on a sideboard and gave it to Hari instructing him to dry his hands, then she retrieved the cloth and bid him to sit on a sofa, which seemed to absorb him almost entirely in its thick soft folds.

'Now,' she said, perching daintily on a chair opposite Hari, 'I want you to make sure you are sitting comfortably and are fully relaxed.' Hari nodded, 'Now close your eyes and follow my words carefully.' Hari closed his eyes and nodded again, 'I am going to describe a setting, then I will leave you to let it evolve, and afterwards I shall ask you to explain to me what you have experienced. Do you understand?' Once more Hari nodded.

'It is springtime. You are in a field amidst rolling hills. The grass is a full, rich dark green and all the flowers of the meadow are coming into bloom. The air is wonderfully fresh and clear. You are sitting looking out at all this from beside a huge solitary tree, just into leaf. It may be an oak, a beech, whatever you choose, but it is an outstanding example of its kind.'

She paused for the scene to become established in Hari's mind, then continued, 'You are being slowly enveloped by a beautiful sphere of light, like a bubble. What colour is it?'

'Green.' Said Harry, in a trance-like voice.

'The bubble lifts you gently into the air, and you are floating weightless over the meadow.' She pauses for about 15-seconds, then goes on, 'Now you are being lowered into a handsome garden. The bubble you are in touches the ground and gradually evaporates. The air is filled with perfume from the flowers. You are feeling marvellously happy and well. Not a single thing troubles you. Blossoms and greenery are everywhere. You begin walking along a path between borders abundant with all your favourite plants…'

'Soon you come to an amphitheatre, which flows with attractive creepers and roses; whole multitudes of exotic flora cascade around. There is someone else nearby who you cannot yet see but whose presence delights you, as indeed it should. It is no less than your very own spirit guide…'

Here Madam Rashdi stops talking. It is clear to her that Hari is completely absorbed in his new situation, and that it is beginning to develop of itself like a story. She sits quietly and waits. Shortly, she is aware that a strange silent dialogue is taking place between Hari and his guide.

Madam Rashdi's methods have been refined over centuries and her skills over decades. Her ability to remove her subjects from all thoughts not associated with the scenario she presents is exemplary. Yet she knows that with a little patience and practice Hari will soon no longer need her intervention. He will be at liberty to enter similar scenarios alone at will. She is quite aware that all he needs is a calm setting, half-an-hour – or perhaps an-hour at most - during which he will not be disturbed, and the knowledge that she has just provided. She knows that no matter what a person's background, no matter the turmoil or tranquillity of their circumstances, the experience is open to everyone.

And that inner silent voice, or spirit guide, which is so intimately acquainted with every detail and nuance of the huge iceberg of mind - of which the conscious is merely the exposed peak – can freely commune and, over time, reveal all that is necessary to move towards balance and ultimately to perfect inner harmony and contentment.

8

You Can't Be Serious?

SOME PEOPLE DON'T watch, listen to or read the news because it's mostly negative. Apparently, they prefer not to know what's going-on in the world, especially bad things like hurricanes, floods and wars and so on. There's nothing they can do about them, they say, so why let such events drag you into a gloomy frame of mind?

But why do we care about issues beyond our control? At least, why do we care to the extent of it affecting our mood? If we watch a film or TV drama of a fictional war, does that affect us negatively?

From '*The Colossus of Maroussi*' (1941)
by Henry Miller

> "*I would set out in the morning and look for new coves and inlets in which to swim. There was never a soul about. I was like Robinson Crusoe on the island of Tobago. For hours at a stretch I would lie in the sun doing nothing, thinking of nothing. To keep the mind empty is a feat, a very healthful feat too. To be silent the whole day long, see no newspaper, hear no radio, listen to no gossip, be thoroughly and completely lazy, thoroughly and completely indifferent to the fate of the world is the finest medicine a man can give himself. The book-learning gradually dribbles away; problems melt and dissolve; ties are gently severed; thinking, when you design to indulge in it, becomes very primitive; the body becomes a new and wonderful instrument; you look at plants or stones or fish*

with different eyes; you wonder what people are struggling to accomplish by their frenzied activities; you know there is a war on but you haven't the faintest idea what it's about or why people should enjoy killing one another; you look at a place like Albania - it was constantly staring me in the eyes - and you say to yourself, yesterday it was Greek, today it's Italian, tomorrow it may be German or Japanese, and you let it be anything it chooses to be. When you're right with yourself it doesn't matter what flag is flying over your head or who owns what or whether you speak English or Monongahela. The absence of newspapers, the absence of news about what men are doing in different parts of the world to make life more livable or unlivable is the greatest single boon...."

If only we could train ourselves to adopt this kind of emotional indifference to what we can't influence - and Instead, like Miller, focus our emotional responses on our immediate field of activity (or repose – as in the above example). Engage the intellect by all means - but reserve emotions for what you choose or have influence over.

Many people are inclined to take things too seriously. My greatest bugbear is losing or misplacing some item or other. What's yours? If you get nudged in a crowd and someone swears at you, or if hooted at in your car by an impatient driver, or by a slow driver you overtake... then why not smile back, at least smile inside to yourself? You know that's the best way to 'play-the-game', the most beneficial for you, for feeling good: to refuse to become niggled by trivia. If you spill a glass of milk.... it's done, just take it from there and do what's necessary.

t's easy for me to write these ideas, but the only way to move nto avoiding useless anger, gloom or stress is to practice what Miller managed to achieve: that is, being completely in 'the NOW'. The key word here is 'practice', just as you'd practice playing a violin if you aimed to master it. True, at first the performance will be lousy with feeble timing and wrong notes, but it's a start. And, as the old saying goes: every journey begins with a single step.

So remember: don't reflect on the negative after a minor event, but instead bring yourself into the NOW and go forward with it (even if the now is negative, just stay with it without reflection - and if you can do that, then you'll act appropriately too). Above all: smile inside - remember: you're glad to be alive…. it's not that important, you say to yourself as you relax and move forward, it's not life-or-death nor the end-of-the-world. It's merely a little hiccup that tomorrow will be ancient history. And besides, aren't there's more important issues to attend to…. like finding a surprise gift for my best friend?

9

A Chance Episode

MANY YEARS AGO in the early days of Channel-4, on a cool autumn evening when no-one else was about - and I had nothing better to do (luckily) - I sat down and perchance watched a 2-hour documentary on the life of a Buddhist monk. Normally this programme would have bored me out of my head, but I suppose I happened to be in just the right frame of mind - otherwise I'd have soon switched off or changed channels.

As is generally known, there are many variations of Buddhism, each following a different kind of route through life, but mostly with more-or-less similar aims and outlooks. These I have failed to study in any detail, so although I've casually read several books on Buddhism and related issues - both fiction and non-fiction - I cannot claim to speak with authority. (The same goes for most subjects - even, I dare say, 'idling').

But that 2-hour documentary was certainly thought-provoking - if for no other reason than that it was real and live for me at the time, as though I witnessed something both simple and natural but also profound. The monk being filmed - and there was only this one youthful (yet middle aged) solitary guy throughout - lived as a hermit in a little wooden hut high in the Tibetan mountains (at least, that's where I think it was). Surrounded by fabulous views, among trees and loose scree, he carried out his daily activities, few that they were, in complete serenity, so it seemed, and with an enviable childlike joy. The only sounds were ambient: of his movements, of birds, the wind in the trees and so on.

Every few minutes, however, he made a brief comment in his own language - and an accompanying subtitle translation would appear bottom of screen. So intrigued by the first several minutes of this - even before the monk had uttered a word - that as soon as he spoke, which took me by complete surprise, I grabbed a pencil and paper (which by amazing good fortune just happened to be close by) and copied down what he said.

Although, I believe, the film actually spanned pretty well a whole day from dawn to dusk, somehow - which I suppose signifies the astute way his mind worked - the monk's intermittent discourse falls together as one integrated piece. His words seemed to spell out what to me was only vaguely intelligible. That is, I had the impression afterwards that anyone who understood these things would make clear sense of the discourse - which appears to dwell, as one might expect, on the most pressing matters of existence: life and death. Every time I read these 586 words, I experience a taste of the surreal, of the mysterious, of the sublime - as well as, I have to say, continuing puzzlement: for it's like looking across an immense ocean, at the waves, the sky and clouds, the sun even, beaming with all its unfathomable glory - all relatively simple and familiar things - but seeing nothing of what the ocean actually is and contains as might be discovered in the depths and vastness beneath its surface. There were long silences between sentences - providing time to muse... but see how it comes across to you. (The title is mine):

THOUGHTS OF A SAGE

There is no beginning and no end.

Worldly feelings lead to entanglements and anguish. In the end one loses what one loves. That's why one experiences pain. You have no entanglements so you have no pain. You must employ your soul and wash away your anguish. To understand that worthlessness is worthless - that is the pathway to the Buddha.

Now be silent - I will introduce you to a master armed with the power of the law who will open your eyes and show you the way. Free the moon hidden inside you and it will light the sky and the earth. Its light will chase away all the shadows of the universe. Understand that one thing and you will understand everything. Achieve this and the good news will echo through the universe. It will be total perfection. All will be accomplished. There will be no obstacles. Freedom will prevail.

When the moon in one's heart wells up through the water, where does the master of one's being go? If you meditate on this single-mindedly day and night, concentrating your entire being on the puzzle, you will reach Enlightenment without fail. The Koan is a tool to cross the sea of anguish and illusion so as to discover the roots of the true Self.

What is the non-difference between birth and death? What is the non-difference between Self and Other?

Hoping to shake myself free from the dust and dirt of the world and seek perfection, I became a hermit. But then I realised life's passions, the dirt and the dust and even life's hardships. Without loving them it was impossible to reach perfection. This is because perfection means embracing all things. It may be easy to fight against reality and fate, but it is difficult to love them. How beautiful the world is when you know how to love it. The world is not imperfect - rather the imperfection is in our language and knowledge - it is simply that our consciousness is insufficient.

Is Enlightenment anything but a dream? Trusting in Enlightenment alone I left the world, but when I look back on the things I sacrificed they fall upon me like demons and fill me with bitterness. I was afraid I would fall into an endless hell of remorse. What does 'Save Humanity' mean? We, relying on Enlightenment alone, leave all our family and obligations, but for what? Who is Buddha and who is not? Isn't it said that there is no Buddha and no unenlightened creature? I am going back to the world, to the turbulence of life.

Mountains, rivers, plants, the universe. Here, there, everywhere - all things lie within the same enclosure. To leave is to arrive. To arrive is to leave. Doesn't the wind blow as it pleases from all points of the compass?

I am insubstantial in the universe, but, in the universe, there is nothing that is not me. When the body is scattered, where does the master of one's being go?

The formula which destroys hell is:

Once you shake off the dream, you reach Enlightenment. All around is deep in shadow. Light the wick in your heart and illuminate your own path. Winter advances through the dense forest. Summer creeps up on the naked branches. In the cycle without beginning or end, to live or die are the same thing. But life is for those who stay. In the unending eternal stream there is no birth and no death. But for those who stay, death is an insoluble problem.

.
.
.
.
.

10

Studs Terkel

WHEN IT WAS ANNOUNCED that Studs Terkel had died (Oct 2008) I looked-up his extensive work on Amazon - all of which had excellent reviews - one guy had written, intriguingly:

> "Great Book - I read this book 30 years ago. It has probably kept me unemployed for most of that time. Warning: if you read this book you may quit your job."

Here's an extract from the synopsis for that volume, '*Working: People Talk About What They Do All Day and How They Feel About What They Do*':

> "There is hardly an interviewer, commentator or probing journalist among us who can elicit so much grief and passion, so many forlorn hopes and decayed dreams, so much of the tedium and frustration of daily existence from his subjects as Studs Terkel. Subjects? Hardly. Talking casually, sometimes disjointedly and hesitantly, or unleashing long suppressed feelings in an angry torrent, these are not clinical case studies but complex, fully human people whose humdrum reminiscences of long hours, days and years on the job are almost painfully involving. Even their laughter, abrupt and nervous, will make you wince because in Terkel's words, "This book, being about work is, by it's very nature, about violence - to the spirit as well as to the body." "You're nothing more than a machine. . . . They give better care to that machine than they will to you. They'll have more respect, give more attention to that machine," says the twenty-seven

year-old spot welder at Ford. "I'm a mule" says the steelworker. Nor is the sense of waste and futility confined to blue-collar workers. Terkel talks to shipping clerks and sports figures, copy boys, hospital aides, salesmen, press agents, a doorman, a barber, a fireman, a cop, a pharmacist, a piano tuner, a stockbroker, a gravedigger. . . and yes, there is a common chord. Pride, the pride of craftsmanship is harder and harder to sustain; the old work ethic seems to many like a dirty trick."

A constant source of puzzlement to me is that so many people who are well-off enough to stop working, decide instead to continue the other-directed (and essentially arbitrary) activity - frequently tedious or unpleasant - that has already claimed so much of their lives. How is it that so many people are incapable of recognising the benefits, and taking the initiative, of redirecting their lives towards permanent freedom – that is, to choose themselves, instead of obeying others, how to spend their limited time in the oasis - and to enjoy the far more worthwhile existence that accompanies it?

Most people, unless they're prepared to live at subsistence level, are too poor to escape the tedium of work and have no choice but to join the treadmill at some point or other.

But many more people than do, could afford to throw-in their job tomorrow if they chose, and could thereby begin at last to benefit from life in what it really has to offer. That so many people defer for as long as possible the great luxury of freedom which we are all supposedly working towards - in favour of the mind-numbing grind the elite who rule over us have ordained - represents a kind-of mass paralysis, a mass betrayal of heritage.

Why do so many people find it so hard to break from their 'shackles' - shackles as ephemeral, in fact, as fairy-dust - shackles of such obvious lies and propaganda that they were programmed as infants to obey: the work ethic the elite have ordained? It is a travesty in the first place that kids are stuffed with this work ethic: of motivating and driving oneself, of having to achieve, compete, outshine and outpace one's neighbours - and swindle them into the bargain if one can (after all, isn't that the implicit nature of capitalism: to exploit any opportunity to profit, buying-and-selling, 'investing'?). Isn't it the greatest travesty of all that this humbug is drummed into people so young, as though it's the principal purpose of life which should take precedence and be pursued above all else?

Well, that brief indented comment above (ie, '*Great book-*") suggests that the efforts of the great Studs Terkel went some way towards correcting this perennial curse.

It's even worse for kids who are victim also to religious bunkum - is there anything in religion that isn't bunkum? Christianity, so called, has these days (especially in the US) become so reactionary that if Jesus ever existed (and hadn't risen into heaven) he'd be spinning in his grave. Likewise, I suspect, Islam in Islamic countries.

Why do we feel compelled to shove so much humbug into the heads of infants - humbug we can so obviously see that, except for the most astute, will later only spoil or even destroy their chances of ever growing into free-thinking individuals? Why do we insist on burdening them with the corruptions, hang-ups and outworn follies of a dying generation that has made such a monumental cock-up of the world, and should be forced to take all their bilge with them to the grave? Why?

As Kurt Vonnegut so poignantly pronounced shortly before he died:

> "*A message for the new generation: I hope you'll forgive us.*"

Although we inherit the previous generation's faulty genes, they don't count for much in developing our skills for observation and discrimination in what we retain of theirs - and discard what is so clearly trash: ie: first, the notion that we

HAVE TO work, compete, excel, and so on - and second, that we HAVE TO believe in any supernatural mumbo-jumbo.

You only have to examine it to see that almost all of what we inherit is about maintaining the status quo. Some of this is to our benefit, but most is for the benefit of a ruthless ruling elite that holds power over us all and intends, come what may, to retain it.

* * * * *

Despite lessons from Studs Terkel, we still have to lead our lives in the material world where there are certain requirements to fulfil if we want to find contentment and meaning.

Here's some notes from *'The Master Game'* (1968) by Robert de Ropp (1968):

> '...It has been stated by Thomas Szasz that what people really need and demand from life is not wealth, comfort or esteem but GAMES WORTH PLAYING. He who cannot find a game worth playing is apt to fall prey to accidie - a paralysis of the will, a failure of the appetite, a condition of generalised boredom, total disenchantment: "...how weary, stale, flat and unprofitable seem to me all the uses of this world!" Such a state of mind, Szasz tells us, is a prelude to what is loosely called "mental illness," which, though Szasz defines this illness as a myth, nevertheless fills half the beds in hospitals and makes multitudes of people a burden to themselves and society.'

> 'Seek, above all, for a game worth playing. Such is the advice of the oracle to modern man. Having found the game, play it with intensity - play it as if your life and sanity depended on it. (They do depend on it.) Follow the example of the French existentialists and flourish a banner bearing the word "engagement". Though nothing means anything and all roads are marked "NO EXIT," yet move as if your movements had some purpose. If life does not seem to offer a game worth playing, then invent one.

For it must be clear, even to the most clouded intelligence, that any game is better than no game.'

A description of what constitutes a game follows, then a categorisation of the two divergent kinds of game, defined as Object games and Meta games. Which of these suits you, depends on the type of person you are and on your level of inner development, says de Ropp. Object games are those played for the attainment of material things, primarily money and what it can buy. Meta games are played for intangibles such as knowledge or "salvation of the soul". In our culture, object games predominate. In earlier cultures it was meta games. To players of meta games, object games seem shallow and futile, while to players of object games, meta games seem fuzzy and ill-defined. The whole human population can be divided roughly into these two groups of players, the Prosperos and the Calibans. The two have never understood one another, and probably never will, de Ropp continues. They are, psychologically speaking, different species of Man and their conflicts throughout the ages have added greatly to the sum of human misery.

Meta:

Master game – awakening
Religion game – salvation
Science game – knowledge
Art game – beauty

Object:

Hog in trough – wealth
Cock on Dunghill – fame
Moloch game - glory or victory

All this presents yet another angle on our situation in the oasis - one that, whether it previously occurred to us or not, we all surely recognise. I discovered this 250-page book back in the mid eighties and found it impressive, especially the opening chapter, the beginning of which I've summarised above. It explains so much, but what can we learn from it - if, that is, we accept its premise, the principles it asserts, and the implications? Learning is like living, we have to do I for ourselves; no-one can do it for us. This is an excellent task for our amazing brains to examine.

So find your game, if you can. Otherwise keep searching, trying what looks promising- and if that fails, move on, keep searching. Once you've found your game, you're home.

If you need occasional change, then when alone try positive contemplation, observe your surroundings like a Zen master, without judgment - or do something creative, this is always rewarding - or just enjoy the pleasure of idling or some kind of exercise: walking, gardening... even solving intellectual puzzles.

11

Zen

SIMPLICITY - PURITY - NATURALNESS

'...*The aimless life is the constant theme of Zen art of every kind, expressing the artist's own inner state of going nowhere in a timeless moment. We all have these moments occasionally, and it is just then that we catch those vivid glimpses of the world which cast such a glow over the intervening wastes of memory – the smell of burning leaves on a morning of autumn haze, a flight of sunlit pigeons against a thundercloud, the sound of an unseen waterfall at dusk, or the single cry of some unidentified bird in the depths of a forest...*'

From '*The Way of Zen*' by Alan Watts

The implications of Eckhart Tolle's '*The Power of Now*' when taken together with Zen according to that famous old sage D.T. Suzuki - reveal a more powerful perspective on the human predicament than would be possible for either alone.

Although we humans are individual and unique, we have much in common - as most birds, for instance, have much in common despite large differences in behaviour and appearance. The differences between you and me, as human beings, is marginally genetic but much more down to experience - which begins from our moment of birth (possibly before). Observe a native of the UK (me) and compare that with someone from Thailand, Africa or South America - see how beliefs, everyday lives and outlooks differ. Equally, observe someone brought up working-class (me again) and see how that compares with someone from the underclass or middle-class. I am as much tied up with my background of experience as anyone - though I needn't be if I made an effort to extricate myself. And there are several ways of escape, ways I can free myself from the past - or at least from aspects of it I find disagreeable.

For instance, there are methods like: making a clean break, starting a completely new life in another place with new people, etc. and there's such methods as psychoanalysis. Zen, though, is probably the most effective and least disruptive way to relinquish shackles of the past. Even so, there are aspects of Zen that 'seem' beyond reach for me. But this is one of the great qualities of Zen: that it helps us move beyond experience - or you might say: back from it, back into closer proximity to our natural unspoiled state of mind. Eckhart Tolle (in his *The Power of Now*') has a few things to say on this. But his response is only part of the solution. The chief part - I believe - is laid out by Suzuki.

The trouble these days with all the weird alternative religions and cults around the world with their various jargon and rituals and hierarchies and what not, is that for many people in the west *genuine life philosophies* like Zen have become lumped in with them. Those other outfits, though, are invariably parasitic and alien. They often take any opportunity to rope-in the most vulnerable people, who they deviously groom and exploit. And they frequently present rules, rituals and rigmaroles that are a curiously alluring combination of simplicity and baffling illogic.

Zen exists on an entirely different plane. In Zen there is no individual or group who sets out to persuade or convert. There are no rituals, hierarchies or secrets. There is no god or other mysterious supernatural entity. Do you remember observing the world when you were two, three, or even five, say? You knew no names for plants or birds or buildings or aeroplanes. You had no thought of how they worked or why. To you they just were. They, like you, existed in a world or universe that was not in the least mysterious because the concept of mystery did not arise. It was all *just* there and *you* were part of it. But not only *that*: You were also there at that moment; You were always PRESENT.

At some point, as Tolle observes, you began to slide away from this present. In order to avoid undesirable events or, more likely, to blend with the human world around you, tackle abstract issues that increasingly took control of your mind as you transcended childhood, almost all your time was spent away from the present. Instead you focused on the past or future or various abstract and intellectual issues.

Another angle on this is that our human brains have evolved from the single right-brain of most animals. We have a bicameral mind: an intuitive right-brain and an intellectual left-brain. But we can't simply switch-off our calculating, reflecting, projecting left-brain and rely on our (in-the-moment) 'animal' right brain as we might imagine. Even if we could, can we be sure it would be of benefit? Questions arise like: Do animals have compassion, or lament when sad - at the death of a mate, for instance? Aren't these responses dependent on left-brain attributes: the conscious ability to look back or ahead?

Many animals do show distress at such times, yet how is this possible if they lack the intellectual left-brain that enables reflections or projections? Ouspensky called living in the present 'self-remembering'. Eckhart Tolle seems to concentrate predominately on the 'self' with regard to this - the 'I' that stands above our thinking mind and observes it in action, both intuition and intellect: its calculating, reflecting, emotion like anger or happiness or its just BEING - which is probably the IDEAL untainted reality from which we can relate to and react with the world.

In waveguide technology: for maximum power transfer from a waveguide to an aerial the impedances of both must be the same. Obeying this particular law of physics/nature means the system is optimised. So we adjust the length (impedance) of the guide to match the aerial. Now there will be no reflections to cause interference, nor any power loss or wasted energy. Maybe you could say the waveguide and the aerial love one another... though I guess that's a bit weird for inanimate things. But it's how you get the best possible reception. And I'd imagine it's the same with your MIND: Its best - *its optimum* - mode is probably when held in the present so one's attention is not scattered wastefully - though (if appropriate) one is *aware* of past and future - *AND* at the same time in tune with surroundings: only naming or analysing when necessary for a particular task.

This focus on the present concurs with Eugen Herrigel's experience as i interpret it in the next item. Hence to remain, I suggest, as far as possible in the (optimum) Zen mode: stay in the present, observe from above your mind, alert to surroundings as they really are (not intellectualised, unbiased by mood or irrational influence), AND in any action or decision: elevate compassion above every other consideration. In short: be PRESENT, be AWARE, be COMPASSIONATE.

Are these rules? No - not man-made, at any rate - because like for the waveguide, nature has certain conditions that it is our disadvantage to ignore. The addition of compassion means that Karma too is optimised: we will be left with an untainted conscience. (A tainted conscience might be analogous to stray reflections in a waveguide that interfere with the signal).

Here's an intriguing little Zen parable that illustrates the Zen approach, which I think is worth a moment or two of contemplation:

IS THAT SO?

> *The Zen master Hakuin was praised by his neighbours as one living a pure life.*
> *A beautiful Japanese girl whose parents owned a food store lived near him. Suddenly, without any warning, her parents discovered she was with child.*

This made her parents angry. She would not confess who the man was, but after much harassment at last named Hakuin.

In great anger the parents went to the master. 'Is that so?' was all he would say.

After the child was born it was brought to Hakuin. By this time he had lost his reputation, which did not trouble him, but he took very good care of the child. He obtained milk from his neighbours and everything else the little one needed.

A year later the girl-mother could stand it no longer. She told her parents the truth - that the real father of the child was a young man who worked in the fishmarket.

The mother and father of the girl at once went to Hakuin to ask his forgiveness, to apologize at length, and to get the child back again.

Hakuin was willing. In yielding the child, all he said was'. 'Is that so?'

From: *'Zen Flesh, Zen Bones'*

FROM HOWARD ZINN (1922- 2010):

"To be hopeful in bad times is not just foolishly romantic, it is based on the fact that human history is a history not only of cruelty, but also of compassion, sacrifice, courage, kindness -- and if we do act, in however small a way, we don't have to wait for some grand utopian future. The future is an infinite succession of presents, and to live now, as we think human beings should live, in defiance of all that is bad around us, is itself, a marvelous victory."

Zinn's quote might look a bit incongruous here, appearing immediately after that eye-opening little parable. But most of us remain quite a distance from where that parable goes, while the concept of hope/desire informs a significant part of our human psyche... a concept - unlike the detachment implied in the parable - that we readily empathise with. The fact remains, though, that ultimately "our only hope is to abandon hope" - a notion that's almost (?) a koan... another huge and intriguing aspect of Zen...

HERRIGEL

Eugen Herrigel's world famous book '*Zen in the Art of Archery*' introduced me some decades ago to a completely new way of observing and approaching life. Not that I practiced it enough to be able to adopt the Zen approach more than on occasions when it occurred to me to do so, when it might be useful or delightful, say.

I've never even attempted archery - in the practical sense - as a professional archer frequently does. But this doesn't matter. The particular activity, to which Herrigel's philosophy and approach applies, is really irrelevant. It's maybe three or four decades since I read this little book - which can be devoured in one sitting (and contemplated for a lifetime) - but its key feature, as I recall, is that you are taken right into the very nub of the action... you focus down to the most minuscule detail of only what is immediate. And even then, it's not a question of concentration - but rather about poise, being relaxed, natural, at one with '*what is*'. At the point of the arrow's release, the archer doesn't even consider the target - which might seem absurd. Yet there's an invaluable lesson here. It's a lesson about observing, about becoming like plasticine, allowing your mind to shape around the situation, to exactly fit '*what is*': the 'true reality' in every sense and at that very instant. An analogy might be the way you let your eyes relax so they can find their own focus on those 3D computer pictures that are otherwise an unintelligible mass of repeating coloured patterns. I was convinced that as a philosophy Herrigel had cracked a great secret. And I'm reminded of the Zen story '*Is That So?*' in which, instead of resisting or attempting to fight as anyone normally might, the Zen master Hakuin knows better: he flexes and moves with the wind, the conditions, deflecting and adjusting... one moment this... next moment that... unhesitatingly according with circumstances... precisely as illustrated by Alan Watts in '*The Watercourse Way*' and D T Suzuki in his '*Studies in Zen*'.

Unfortunately - like so much else in life unless one makes a great effort to embrace a thing - the practice of Zen, as I say, is not something I've done very much. The times when it's been especially useful is at moments of impasse. Then, poised and focused, a new perspective appears which can be immensely illuminating... like 'lateral thinking', I've found, it becomes immediate and automatic, and everything falls into place as best it possibly could, or so it seems: as though decisions/actions are optimised.

A recent radio programme explained how people who suffer depression experience an excess of continual and unquenchable brain activity: (ie, random chatter). This can apparently be reduced by electro-therapy - which is a help to most, though not all, sufferers. Perhaps, instead, one could try deliberate poise and then focus as described above – on what you're doing or ideally to focus on nothing, though a candle or any simple object or even a mantra could be used. See chapter-6 for my approach as was touched-on - perhaps, in fact, much more than merely touched-on - in a Theosophy Course I attended some years ago. Spurred by Herrigel's book, I write the following:

ZEN in the ART of IDLING

That might be the title of a book that can't exist because what would anyone capable of writing a book on anything know about idling? Yet I claim to be quite a well-practiced idler myself. Besides which, as we've seen in chapter-8, although Henry Miller was no idler, he definitely knew how to idle.

So maybe a thousand or so words is possible. Taking a Zen perspective might strike you as a bit weird at first, but dipping-in on a few examples shows it can be very worthwhile. Some literature on the subject seems to contradict the kind of impression of Zen given above - which portrays Zen as a generally inactive philosophy, a kind-of perception of the world someone might have if they were completely calm and composed with a fresh uncritical and unbiased mind.

In contrast, there are some who might regard it as an active philosophy: a way of achieving authentic action (as opposed to inaction) ... specifically in this instance as applied to idling. These two angles ('inactive' and 'active') are not inconsistent though.

Authentic action (or inaction), incidentally, is achieved when every aspect of mind-&-body is focussed (or blank), with no stray or irrelevant thoughts to distract from that. This allows the mind, at least in theory, to focus exclusively on every aspect possible of the current situation and to respond in the most expedient way taking everything into account: whether at the scene of a car crash or sitting alone on a beach watching the sea.

Some authors on Zen expand on its basic application as described in *'Zen in the Art of Archery',* which, as I say, is not so much about archery but rather - using archery as a metaphor, as a vehicle - about how to take a Zen approach in any (in)activity - indeed, to life in general.

As ever, we have to assess these things for ourselves according to what feels appropriate, which will depend on one's own unique way of thinking, experience of life, etc – which changes with time. Some people find Zen outstanding, and practice it in their everyday life to great personal advantage. Most of us get by OK without it.

As I see it, Zen operates on an elevated level of consciousness (or awareness) from where you can observe yourself being what you are and doing what you're doing. This higher 'self', which unlike the rest of your mind remains, as I've described, identical from birth to death, is unaffected by learning and by preconceptions or prejudices, moods or circumstances, happiness, anger, contentment or gloom, wealth or poverty etc., etc., and is completely in tune with the reality you're in, which the rest of your mind usually isn't.... unless you've been practicing Zen (or something like it) for some while.

The famous Hamlet cigar advert comes to mind where all around is in turmoil, buildings collapsing etc., then the guy in the picture lights a Hamlet cigar and everything fades into the background so he smiles contentedly. I guess cannabis might have a similar effect, though also and more effectively would Zen - except with Zen if any action is needed the guy would act, whereas in the advert the cigar has made him oblivious, placed now in a kind-of dream-world of pure idleness.

All this means that by using the Zen perspective you're able to detach yourself from irrational thoughts, disabling emotions or disturbing conditions because you now observe them from a distance, so to speak, so see them for what they truly are. Moreover, you're not only detached, but at the same time – as a kind-of bonus – you're able to deal with any situation in the most all-round beneficial way... untainted by irrational aspects of thought, etc... like Hakuin in the little Zen story above *'Is That So?'*, which is a fine illustration of Zen in practice.

The story demonstrates how an apparently idle approach forms the essence of poise. So Hakuin, by adopting the idle mode, achieves perfection. That's the theory... or part of it. Some of us would judge Hakuin as caving-in, too idle to confront an injustice. But that must be judged as Hakuin's personal choice, his calculation taking everything around him and in his life into account. His decision lands him with much work looking after the infant, whereas by confronting his accusers and refusing their claims his home-life would have remained unchanged. But what about his inner life? Your calculation in that moment of poise when your mind is at rest, weighing in that moment all the aspects appropriate to you and your particular circumstances, may be otherwise – we are all different, as too is our state of affairs. We assess a situation subconsciously in almost an instant, like an instinctive response, but with the whole situation as we understand it with all of our brain engaged.

If we do this from a Zen position then, according to the theory at least, we make the most wise decision resulting in the best possible outcome. This might appear at first to be a bad decision to an observer. But how many examples of 'received-wisdom', 'tradition' etc., demonstrate negative consequences ultimately from failing to take a Zen position? I could list many: from some trivial personal angst to international catastrophes.

For instance, A S Neil, famous for Summerhill school and his revolutionary psychology in helping children with antisocial behaviour to transcend their troubled condition, gave small amounts of money to kids who stole money. Traditionalists would have punished the kid and exacerbated the situation, whereas Neil both solved the problem and helped the kids become social.

Prison is a perfect example of authority scoring an own-goal. The Zen approach would be vastly more beneficial all round. Spending tax money on providing a good start in life for all children would save colossal amounts later from reduced medical costs, benefits costs, etc. A Zen approach to rules that are intended to reduce climate change would be vastly more effective than at present.

Many aspects of life can be so influenced for the better from applying a Zen approach. It's entirely up to us to decide for ourselves whether to practice this, when it might be most appropriate. I think we should always question 'received wisdom' and be alert to 'group-think' and the follies that result from it.

We live and learn, and crucially should look at ourselves sometimes and assess whether what we're doing, what we're involved with is good for us. Never mind others for the moment if you're struggling: you really have to learn to love yourself, and treat yourself as if you do, before you can love others. This is something above all to practice.

12

Going Wild

MANY PEOPLE DELIGHT in observing animals in the wild, in their natural habitat rather than in a zoo or some kind of cage or within a boundary. Bird-watching is particularly popular, maybe because it's so easy to do wherever you are. But one reason for this, I believe, is that wild animals in their natural surroundings and conditions usually, if not always, operate in way that can be truly described as 'free', unencumbered by psychological issues as we humans and domestic animals nearly always are.

Appropriate to this is an essay by Hermann Hesse that I often reflect on:

> "THERE is one virtue that I love, and only one. I call it self-will. - ...True, all the virtues man has devised for himself might be subsumed under a single head: obedience. But the question is: whom are we to obey? For self-will is also obedience. But all the other virtues, the virtues that are so highly esteemed and praised, consist in obedience to man-made laws. Self-will is the only virtue that takes no account of these laws. A self-willed man obeys a different law, the one law I hold absolutely sacred - the law in himself, his own 'will'.
>
> It is a great pity that self-will should be held in such low esteem! Do men think well of it? Oh no, they regard it as a vice or at best as a deplorable aberration. They call it by its eloquent full name only where it arouses antagonism and hatred. (Come to think of it, true virtues

always arouse antagonism and hatred. Witness Socrates, Jesus, Giordano Bruno, and all other self-willed men.)...

There are only two poor accursed beings on earth who are excluded from following this eternal call and from being, growing, living, and dying as an inborn and deeply ingrained self-will commands. Only man and the domestic animals he has tamed are condemned to obey, not the law of life and growth, but other laws that are made by men and from time to time broken and changed by men. And the strangest part of it is that those few who have disregarded these arbitrary laws to follow their own natural law have come to be revered as heroes and liberators - though most of them were persecuted in their lifetime. The same mankind which praises obedience to its arbitrary laws as the supreme virtue of the living reserves its eternal pantheon for those who have defied those laws and preferred to die rather than betray their 'self-will'."

Do we envy the wild animals we love to observe – for what we see as their freedom? They live according to their so-called 'right-brain', the instinctive, intuitive brain. We have that too, but we're dominated, so it seems (??), by our intellectual 'left-brain'. If we could only control which part of our brain to use appropriate to the moment, then maybe we too could be even more free than those wild animals we watch performing as they have for millions of years.

Living by the sea as I do with cliffs and gulls and so on, I once made my own feeble attempt to describe how I perceived as 'great wisdom' what is actually pure instinct. Perhaps this is what bird-watchers do subconsciously: imbue the birds with our intellectual interpretation of instinct as freedom or wisdom, as is often done with animals in books for children.

The Seagull (a prose poem)

As I stand on the cliff-top looking west my thoughts dissolve, and for a moment I'm really there, held in a timeless paradise. Below, the rugged ground descends into a broad glen covered with bushes and trees. To my left a sheer drop to the sparkling blue ocean with its tiny distant waves lapping and foaming along the shore. On the far side of the glen another cliff, another view, another paradise.

Gulls swoop and glide above my head. Across the glen they go then back again, screeching joyfully as they plummet and soar, coasting upwards, proud and triumphant, relishing each precious instant in private celebration. An hour from now it will be the same, and tomorrow, and next year, as it has been for aeons. Suspended in perpetual glory, agile, graceful, diving, climbing, floating, circling, endlessly dancing to some eternal secret tune.

I gaze down through quivering tufts of grass clinging stubbornly to the cliff face, and there below I see the many-coloured boulders, rocks and fine scree upon which the waves are breaking: yellows, browns and pinks – and do I see orange too?

The moment passes; my dreary thoughts return. Tomorrow I'll be in the city, jostled in crowds, gasping in fumes, assaulted by noise, bored by tedious work. Shall I remember the gulls? Shall I remember my moment in paradise?

I look up once more. The gulls still hover above my head and drift silently now across the lush, thick glen. One of these splendid birds floats down and lands on a nearby post; leaning his head to one side, he stares towards me. His feathers ruffle in the warm breeze. I feel he is trying to tell me something. It is something important, he seems to say, but there is no hurry, you'll find out... you'll find out sooner or later. He opens his wings and rises, slowly, effortlessly, still looking at me, now with sorrow, now with joy, and he is gone. Across the glen he goes. Up high he mingles with his kin and I lose sight of him, my momentary friend; I shall not forget you with your kind eyes, your great wisdom, your elusive message.

Yes, I'll find out.

By interpreting the seagull's natural activity, its relaxed, easy manner as though playing around in the air just for the joy of it, as I might sprint and leap and weave along the sand at low tide, without a care, without even a thought, operating on auto, as it were... by observing the gull as I did seemed to transfer to my subconscious some of that freedom/wisdom that I rendered to the gull.`

The gull would have been 'in the moment' and probably observed me as a potential hazard, something to keep a distance from even if it was curious to see me close-up – though I've read that birds have the most amazing vision, with eyes vastly superior to ours. I don't doubt it.

But the key here is in returning to our natural state, as we were when very young. Hermann Hesse enjoyed his youth, or at least the protagonist in one of his best stories did, and tries to return to it. I guess it's a story of nostalgia, of how we felt before we became corrupted by all kinds of attractions and diversions that only removed us further from what really counts in life.

Hesse's *'The Journey to the East*' is perhaps his most poignant work. And we can easily relate to it, for each of our lives is a journey, sometimes smooth, bathed in sunshine and adorned with flowers... sometimes rough and barren, festooned with stones beneath turbulent skies. But although he sets us going in leaps, one soon realises that Hesse's journey was exclusively his own, and can belong to no-one but him. Like Leo in *'The Journey to the East*', we suddenly realise we have lost our way, and just as Leo seeks to return to his lost 'path', so can we.

On the back of my copy of *'The Journey to the East*' is written:

"...is the story of a youthful pilgrimage that seemingly failed. As the book opens, the narrator is engaged in writing the chronicle of this remembered adventure - the central experience of his youth. As he becomes immersed in retelling the chronicle, the writer realises that only he has failed, that the youthful pilgrimage continues in a shining and mysterious way."

It's impossible to avoid falling under the spell, of believing that this is all our chronicles, that we all have failed, but that unknown to us, because of our adult blindness - caused by years of becoming increasingly lost, of unrelenting diversions from what we inwardly know should be our true course if only we had the courage to follow it - unknown to us, the great universal pilgrimage goes on; we have only to open our eyes... Luckily, the book is small, about 100 pages, because I confess that I had to read it several times before I began to sense its significance.

See Appendix for Hesse's prose poem *'Trees'*. A psychologist I met in Auckland youth hostel New Zealand three decades ago reckoned *'Trees'* was a small masterpiece that could help many people burdened with some kind of self-loathing or diminished condition. Not only does it show the appropriateness of accepting ourselves totally as we are, faults, foibles, whatever, but that to recognise and grasp the strengths a troubled past has given us helps us to escape it to become uplifted and optimistic.

.
.
.
.
.

13

Change Your Mind

IT IS TRUE THAT there have been times when I've felt sad, gloomy, unhappy... but never have my circumstances been so bad that I'd have failed to laugh at some quip that touched my sense of humour. But then, crucially, I've never felt in any kind of jail. I've never been stuck in a situation that I couldn't escape from – except when on a boat, aircraft, or motorway.... none of which confine one for very long. I could have always walked out of a place of work, a classroom etc.

But a massive detail that consistently evokes gloom that we can't walk away from – and has over the aeons inspired many a futile search for a way out – is the inevitability of death.

Pirandello:

> 'Whoever understands the game can no longer fool themselves, but if you cannot fool yourself, you can no longer derive any pleasure or enjoyment from life. So it goes. My art is full of bitter compassion for all those who fool themselves. But this compassion cannot help but be succeeded by a ferocious derision of a destiny that condemns Man to deception. This, succinctly, is the reason for the bitterness of my art, and also my life.'

So am I fooling myself when I race along the sand at low tide feeling full of the joys of life, not a conscious thought in my head other than what my senses provide, just sensing the air on my face and so on? Of course, unless we attempt to fool ourselves with some kind of supernatural belief, one cannot deny complete demise is our ultimate fate. Not a happy thought, I confess. Even so, the only solution I can see is acceptance – then move-on. We have to accept gravity, our dependence on a constant supply of air and almost constant water.... etc. so maybe we need to regard the inevitability of death in the same way: as just another of the things we have to face.

And that's important... because otherwise – like our non-acceptance of any unalterable fact – we're asking for trouble: ie, depression. At least, this is so according to Dorothy Rowe in her book *'Depression'* (1983).

Why depression had never caught-up with me puzzled me for decades - ever since I reached that age when one reluctantly begins to acknowledge the truth of one's eventual demise. When so many people suffer depression that has no obvious cause - how, I wondered, had I got away with it?

Could it be, I used to think, that what the media tell us is propaganda? Might it all represent some kind of feel-good fake so that we cheerfully, unquestioningly, accept our luck at not suffering, and continue to slave our lives away in blissful ignorance? I'm sure the corporate elite would endorse such methods.

So when I saw Rowe's book I decided for once to look into the great mystery of my 'escape'. The book's subtitle is: *'The Way Out of Your Prison'*.

"Prison?" I thought, "What prison?" The only prison I'd experienced was school and work. And those were just day-prison from where, if things got bad, I could easily abscond.

Ah, but what about the prison in your head? Now this was a new concept for me – except in the philosophical sense: that we are stuck with our heritage and experience, and in our minds have access to nothing else. But if we are all landed with this, isn't to call it a prison a bit solipsistic?

In the book, a patient describes how it's one thing to be trapped in this 'safe' prison, but quite another (and worse) to be forced to emerge and face the 'dangers' of reality. The dangers being, says the book, that the 'reality' in the victim's mind is different from the reality 'out there'. Which means the victim has to change their 'reality' because the reality 'out there' won't or can't change - it is what it is. But this creates uncertainty, continues the book, hence the 'danger'. So to a depressed person, the best they can hope for is a totally predictable world solid with routine and ritual. Which is not only impossible but, I would imagine, excruciatingly dull.

Further on, the book says that when we were children we created a personal myth ('reality') of our future life. This wasn't just for a guiding map, but to bolster our pride (ego?) in response to the insults the world inflicted on our small person, and to give us courage for the journey ahead. Unfortunately (the book goes on), our map is not reality – which means accepting that we are in error, and need to make corrections.

I can relate to that for a whole multitude of minor instances... like when as a small kid I heard my mum asking for a postal order in the post office, and for years afterwards I wondered what a 'post lorder' was. "What's a lorder?" I'd ask people, and they'd just look at me perplexed. Then one day I discovered my mistake and thought it a tremendous joke. In no way did it create any kind of internal conflict. There are hundred of examples... mostly trivial.

Such errors happen every day. What I learned yesterday and formed an opinion on, today I find an alternative angle: perhaps spontaneously, perhaps from some other source of new information, and am obliged to change my opinion or perspective. It seems to me that this is quite normal – without it... well, I'd probably feel like this computer: full of redundant trash because my hard-drive cannot be updated, only added to (which in the case of this computer is revealed as a kind of slowing of search time, a reluctance to work at any kind of a sensible speed: click on an icon, make a cuppa, return, and with luck it might just be ready to go). I'm not a cynic for nothing.

The book then declares: but to admit you are wrong, particularly you who get depressed, is something you find very hard to do. Given the choice (it says), you would prefer to be *right and suffer* than *wrong and happy*. (the book's italics). Being wrong, it says, creates that dreaded uncertainty (my adjective).

So 'uncertainty' is the enemy. And yet, as we all know, uncertainty is the essence of the world and of life... adaptability, compromise, diversity, improvisation, imagination, creativity... Nothing, except maybe gravity and (unpredictable) CHANGE, is certain. Oh yeah, and death! I wonder if depressed people enjoy that particular certainty: death? Maybe they do? Though if so, where does that leave the ego?

But, I ask, why not have your cake AND eat it? That is: instead of the choice of being *right and suffer* or *wrong and happy* why not be *right and happy*? This is achieved very simply as follows: the instant you perceive that your *right* is in fact *wrong*, instead of turning away as you did in the past, you update it, making it a true *right* - or at least the *rightest right* you can find according to what you know (for it's impossible to know everything)... until what seems a more probable *right* appears, and so on throughout life: which is a constant process of learning, updating, of improved better-informed perception.

Can Dorothy Rowe be correct in this really being how depression arises? Perhaps it's one of many?

In a book *'Sunbathing in the Rain - a cheerful book about depression*' about her own experience of depression, Gwyneth Lewis says that when she asked a therapist what was the real cure of depression, he replied, simply, "Truth!"....We shape our lives, but we're also natural liars and we get things wrong. We can easily live an internal commentary that's a forgery.

Depression is a lie detector. By 'knocking you out' it allows you to revise the way you've been living and perceiving. Most people discern truth without needing this push when they are in error. So if you can get through it - without killing yourself - depression actually becomes a friend, she goes on to say. It teaches you to live in a way that suits you infinitely better. If you fail to listen then it returns with a vengeance, till you get the point.

14

Consciousness and Conscience

THE 'CONSCIOUSNESS' PHENOMENON puzzled me for ages as a kid. It's precisely the kind of mystery that I imagine most kids wonder about at some time or another. I recall reflecting on it during the sombre occasions when, for some minor transgression I'd be chucked out of class at primary school, to stand for what seemed like hours in bleak echoing corridors. What is it, I'd ask myself, about this entity I call 'me' that is so separate and unique and, as for everyone else, so dependent on the most fickle of unlikely circumstances for its coming into existence?

What if it had been someone else? Why is it me? What is it that makes it me? What were the chances of it, whatever it is, being this strange sense I feel called me - and not another (a you)? One might continue on the following tack: after billions of years of evolving galaxies, planetary systems, then Earth, plants and animals forming, and finally, so far, people... and even then the most improbable of fluke situations a mere fraction of which I've alluded to above - could so easily have been otherwise in just one crucial minuscule detail... after all that, here now is this amazing weird unique consciousness I call me? Why? Or more to the point, perhaps, *how*?

Of course, there's no answer to this, nor any of the similar kinds of 'juvenile' questions I used to wonder about: the word 'why' - even frequently the 'how' - is meaningless. It's on the same lines as asking why the universe exists (though 'how', of course, might be another issue).

But conscience too presented a mystery. Also as an infant: why, as I looked-on helpless while an older aggressive kid beat a worm to pulp with a stick, did I feel so anguished? I remember wishing he'd aim the stick at me instead- at least, I could run away.

How, I wondered, could anyone act like that?

Erich Fromm (1900 - 1980) was a psychoanalyst and philosopher who sought to identify the sources of Man's estrangement from himself in western industrialised society:

> ... if we see outer reality as predominately beneficial, then our dreaming will be of less value to us... and vice-versa. By 'reality' is meant culture and the world of humankind, not 'nature' which is neutral (ie, nature is both helpful and dangerous, but intentionally neither 'good' nor 'bad'):

> What differentiates us from the world of animals is our capacity to create culture. What differentiates the higher from the lower stages of human development is the variation in cultural level. The most elementary element of culture, language, is the precondition for any human achievement. Man has been rightly called a symbol-making animal, for without our capacity to speak, we could hardly be called human."

> We learn to think by observing others and by being taught by them. We develop our emotional, intellectual and artistic capacities under the influence of contact with the accumulation of knowledge and artistic achievement that created society. We learn to love and to care for others by contact with them, and we learn to curb impulses of hostility and egoism by love for others, or at least by fear of them.

> Human beings are dependent on each other, they need each other. But human history up to now has been influenced by one fact: material production was not

sufficient to satisfy the legitimate needs of all men. The table was set for only a few of the many who wanted to sit down and eat. Those who were stronger tried to secure places for themselves, which meant that they had to prevent others from getting seats. If they had loved their brothers as much as Buddha or the Prophets or Jesus postulated, they would have shared their bread rather than eat meat and drink wine without them.

But, love being the highest and the most difficult achievement of the human race, it is no slur on man that those who could sit at the table and enjoy the good things of life did not want to share, and therefore were compelled to seek power over those who threatened their privileges.

This power was often the power of the conqueror, the physical power that forced the majority to be satisfied with their lot. But physical power was not always available or sufficient. One had to have power over the minds of people in order to make them refrain from using their fists.

This control over mind and feeling was a necessary element in retaining the privileges of the few.

In this process, however, the minds of the few became as distorted as the minds of the many. The guard who watches a prisoner becomes almost as much a prisoner as the prisoner himself. The "elite" who have to control those who are not "chosen" become the prisoners of their own restrictive tendencies.

Thus the human mind, of both rulers and ruled, becomes deflected from its essential human purpose, which is to feel and to think humanly, to use and to develop the powers of reason and love that are inherent in man and without the full development of which he is crippled.

The consequences of this are starkly clarified by C Wright Mills in his *'The Power Elite'* (1956). Fromm continues:

> *In this process of deflection and distortion man's character becomes distorted. Aims which are in contrast to the interests of his real human self become paramount:*
>
> *His powers of love are impoverished, and he is driven to want power over others. His inner security is lessened, and he is driven to seek compensation by passionate cravings for fame and prestige. He loses the sense of dignity and integrity and is forced to turn himself into a commodity, deriving his self-respect from his saleability, from his success.*
>
> *All this makes for the fact that we learn not only what is true, but also what is false. That we hear not only what is good, but are constantly under the influence of ideas detrimental to life.*
>
> *This holds true for a primitive tribe in which strict laws and customs influence the mind, but it is true also for modern society with its alleged freedom from rigid ritualism. In many ways the spread of literacy and of the media of mass communication has made the influence of cultural clichés as effective as it is in a small, highly restricted tribal culture. Modern man is exposed to an almost unceasing "noise," the noise of the radio, television, headlines, advertising, the movies, most of which do not enlighten our minds but stultify them. We are exposed to rationalizing lies which masquerade as truths, to plain nonsense which masquerades as common sense or as the higher wisdom of the specialist, of double talk, intellectual laziness, or dishonesty which speaks in the name of "honour" or "realism," as the case may be....*
> *Is it surprising, then, that to be awake is not exclusively a blessing but also a curse? Is it surprising that in a state of sleep, when we are alone with ourselves, when we can look into ourselves without being bothered by the noise and nonsense that surround us in the daytime, we are*

better able to feel and to think our truest and most valuable feelings and thoughts?

If these deductions are even partially correct, then it's clear that for the past several millennia we humans have been developing a reality that is not merely alien from the reality we evolved from, but is universally problematic. Furthermore, it is a development that not only distorts our psyche and profoundly influences our dream world, but ultimately portends disaster for humankind - that is, in reality.

It also, if correct, shows that our true inherent nature is not the stupidity and waste, the greed and brutality that so many people have understandably come to believe - but instead what is more in our nature is reason, generosity, love and compassion that our current culture (ie, at least in the West: capitalism) precludes as a predominating force.

15

Ronnie Laing

SOME YEARS AGO browsing second-hand books in the Oxfam shop, I spotted John Clay's 1996 biography of R D Laing. Wherever I dipped-in, I found the book gripping... it was 75p and good as new.

Having over many years collected books that look at least half-promising, I'd read parts of several of Laing's most popular works: ie, *'The Divided Self'*, *'Self and Others'* and especially *'The Politics of Experience AND The Bird of Paradise'*. I say 'especially' because that latter tome contains observations that are perhaps among the most poignant and challenging you're ever likely to contemplate. That is, they question the nature of - the reality behind - human culture as we experience it, understand it and generally accept it... or, as Laing proposes, are conditioned to accept it... frequently to the detriment of our psychological health and much else besides.

The only other times I've seen culture examined to such depth was Paul Bowles' *'The Sheltering Sky'*... and maybe Mark Twain's *'The Mysterious Stranger'*, which parallels Laing's key perceptions. From Clay's biography, I see that Laing was an avid reader in his youth and devoured everything he could from the local library.

Furthermore, what Laing (and Twain) had observed, as in his other books, struck me as manifestly self-evident: eye-opening - and perhaps alarming to some - but undeniably true. Many people, I'm sure, would disagree: that 'reality' should appear that way is not only subjective, but disturbing and dangerously subversive. Yet, from my angle, the self-evidence is entirely objective - essentially scientific: based on clear impartial observation - as I'm sure any anthropologist would confirm.

A quote from Darwin:

> "It is worthy of remark that a belief constantly inculcated during the early years of life, whilst the brain is impressible, appears to acquire almost the nature of an instinct; and the very essence of an instinct is that it is followed independently of reason."

Some people, I well know, cannot 'see' (or even imagine) impartially; their conditioning is total. Hence the controversial reputation Laing's work has acquired in claiming, for instance, that schizophrenia is the consequence of failing to adapt - or perhaps *subconscious refusal* to be conditioned.

In my view the controversy is inappropriate; with regard to applying what Laing discovered, the 'dispute' serves only to deny many potential benefactors treatment that is at worst innocuous, but always benign.

I've yet to understand - now more than half a century after Laing's publications, which are both meticulous and groundbreaking - why they should remain controversial. Here's a paraphrased quote:

> "In the late 1960s Laing gained a reputation for his radical objection to conventional psychiatry. His early book, 'The Divided Self' and 'The Politics of Experience' questioned the right of society to proclaim itself sane and others mad.
>
> Protesting the 'outrageous violence' inflicted on patients by drastic therapies like electric shock, he generated controversy with his willingness to try psychedelic drugs, meditation and other unconventional techniques in search

> *of a healing common ground between doctor and patient."*

Regarding "*..the right of society to proclaim itself sane and others mad.*", from *'The Politics of Experience'* p64:

> *The majority of my own generation did not or do not regard it as stark raving mad to feel it better to be dead than Red. None of us, I take it, has lost too many hours' sleep over the threat of imminent annihilation of the human race and our own responsibility for this state of affairs.*
>
> *In the last fifty years, we human beings have slaughtered by our own hands coming on for one hundred million of our species. We all live under constant threat of our total annihilation. We seem to seek death and destruction as much as life and happiness. We are as driven to kill and be killed as we are to let live and live. Only by the most outrageous violation of ourselves have we achieved our capacity to live in relative adjustment to a civilization apparently driven to its own destruction. Perhaps to a limited extent we can undo what has been done to us, and what we have done to ourselves. Perhaps men and women were born to love one another, simply and genuinely, rather than to this travesty that we can call love. If we can stop destroying ourselves we may stop destroying others. We have to begin by admitting and even accepting our violence, rather than blindly destroying ourselves with it, and therewith we have to realize that we are as deeply afraid to live and to love as we are to die.*

It's frequently the case that innovative and revolutionary ideas or observations evoke hostility, fear and opposition – particularly from those at the forefront of whatever is under the spotlight who'll see any new approach as a challenge, at least to their integrity in failing to have spotted the innovative angle first.

Almost always when this happens, an existing hierarchy will feel threatened: their status, ego and even livelihood are in the balance. This means that established set-ups can be very defensive of their practices, even in the light of the most obvious evidence against them.

As with other 'scientists' (whose work can be proved by independently repeating an experiment or by rigorous mathematics), Laing's approach was also shown to work - yet there was a difference: As he explains in *'The Divided Self'*: unlike a normal clinician who examines a patient as a biological machine and focuses on the broken leg or infected liver, whatever, the psychiatrist needs to treat the patient as a human being, not a machine.

In a revised Preface to *'The Divided Self'* Laing declares that he should have said less in the book about *Them* (the patient) and more about *Us* (the psychiatrist). That is, he is critical of how the profession fails to recognise the significance of the nature of the relationship between psychiatrist and patient and above all of the way the patient is 'treated' - ie, there are many excellent youtubes of Laing.

It was precisely the 'respect', the 'courtesy', as he emphasises so strongly in one video, the way you 'treat' the patient, that formed the foundation of Laing's breakthrough. Often, such patients, with the development of characteristically quirky behaviours, would have likely experienced very little courtesy from anyone, still less from someone with Laing's skills: as he was prepared to do: spending hours just 'being' with the patient, totally there, in silence or - as appropriate - to *really* listen... without distraction, without judgement, criticism, or dishing-out 'wise' advice, etc., etc. (Perhaps Laing was as surprised as anyone that this worked, or worked as well as it did... though I doubt it, because to some of us it looks pretty obvious to me.)

But crucially, it was this kind of early experience that led Laing to challenge the traditional prevailing view that the psychiatrist should regard the patient in the same existential and phenomenological way as a clinician.

There' an 8-min youtube describing one experiment that demonstrates the success of Laing's approach, but which ultimately fails - NOT because of Laing's method of allowing his patients to recover from their trauma naturally, but because once cured they are plunged straight back into the precise circumstances that were the source of, or was exacerbating, their original trauma. ie, a dysfunctional family.

And here's a couple of responses s:

> *Revolutionary psychiatrist R D Laing demonstrates how normal family interactions are selfish and malevolent agendas masquerading as kindness and love, and how such atmospheres produces so called mental illnesses and neuroses. I find it highly distressing that mental health professionals today are unaware of R D Laing and his work.*

> *Yes, I remember it well. One of the best and most informative documentaries ever produced. Always worth a second, third fourth (and so on) watch. This should be compulsory viewing in any educational setting, including religious instruction, natural philosophy and the arts. I have over four decades in developmental, educational and now existential psychology in which Laing's work sits perfectly well. His like are far too rare in the history of academia...*

It's precisely for this that I include R D Laing's work here. It's a clear example of Sartre's 'HELL IS OTHER PEOPLE' – or as my dad used to say *'The helping hand strikes again'*. No-one taking the Zen-mind approach would fail to immediately recognise the falsity of the impasse or paradox here, because when in the NOW and alert to the whole situation, any sort of masquerading - of selfishness and malevolence as kindness and love - would be glaringly obvious.

The first three lines of Auden's *'If I Could Tell You'*, which Laing reads in a video.

> *Time will say nothing but I told you so,*
> *Time only knows the price we have to pay;*
> *If I could tell you I would let you know.*

"If I could turn you, if I could drive you out of your wretched mind, if I can tell you I would let you know."

"These words were written by Dr R D Laing, one of the foremost psychiatrists of our time. Born in Glasgow Scotland in 1927 Laing was drawn at an early age to the misery and suffering he saw around him. Until his death in 1989, he devoted his life to the study of the human condition, redefining our concepts of madness, offering revolutionary humanistic solutions to the problems of mental illness. For Laing modern society imposes prison walls of conformity on the individual, inhibiting potential and devastating the personality. So called Madness may be the result of a person's inability to suppress his normal instincts to conform to an abnormal Society. In exploring what drives people to madness Laing was a master at portraying the incompatible contradictions that can enmesh people in a web of lies and confusions; for him the key to understanding was always personal experience."

Amazon books has some insightful reviews on Laing's *'The Politics of Experience'*:

2017:

I read this book 40 years ago. I have read it again now, realizing how much of my own thinking all through my life has been affected and influenced by this book. My politics, my morality, my understanding of social realities, in fact, of the structure of reality itself, keeps the mark of these extraordinarily radical and intelligent pages. read it.

2016

I have bought this book three times now, it is a seminal works and ought to be made compulsory reading. R D Laing was a phenomenal mind; to the extent, that his works, are not, perhaps, for those who are looking for 'light-reading'. Requires an intelligent mind and a critical one at that. R D Laing deserves a place in history next to Nietzsche, Sartre, Plato.

From Laing's official website:

To this day the life and works of R. D. Laing influence writers, poets, musicians, philosophers, psychologists, therapists, film makers and those involved with the day-to-day challenges of coping and dealing with mental distress.

R.D. Laing was a controversial figure to the Establishment and a hero to the counter-culture movement of the 1960s, which viewed R. D. Laing as a pioneering humanitarian whose works displayed an authentic existential understanding of psychosis.

Scottish existential psychiatrist who argued that insanity could be a creative and adaptive response to the world [and] developed the theory that mental illness was an escape mechanism that allowed individuals to free themselves from intolerable circumstances.

There's no doubt Laing was a remarkable intellect, perhaps a genius; but either way his ideas and perceptions - esp as set-out in *'Politics of Experience'* - reveal aspects of our lives, as I say, that very few people seem to accept, less still are aware of... such is the extent, the depth, the thoroughness of our conditioning. Regarding this, by certain fluke experiences (described in my Memoir), I became aware as a teenager of what Laing describes - among other things. Maybe Laing's early experiences contained similar threads, and with his sharp mind triggered a recognition of the significance of this and other observations he describes? No doubt reading Freud (who I'd scarcely heard of before I was ~30) and others would have honed such observations.

Despite my own incidental recognition of these angles on the human 'predicament', Laing's books have formed quite an eye-opener - if only in the systematic analysis and articulation of key phenomena as I've described.

I'm reminded too of how, as a 14 year-old, I gained an intimate understanding of existentialism (see my Memoir) more than a decade before first hearing the word and being amazed and delighted at finding it to be a popular and major philosophy that I could study. I'd assumed (probably a common error of 14-year olds) my perception to be unique to me - or a view of existence that was taboo (since the prevailing mind-set seemed quite the opposite).

Likewise - above all - witnessing conditions and actions authorities and associated adults created or participated in that to me were not only inexplicable but counterproductive, even hostile.... in other words: my recognition that nearly every aspect of the society I lived in was twisted, apparently irrational and geared to serve some 'mysterious' hierarchical status-quo.... either that or most people were just mad... an observation that Laing must have interpreted as I did, but saw was something to pursue and investigate for its psychological and cultural (more than political) significance.

I say 'mysterious' because I merely accepted it - grudgingly, true, but I made no attempt to understand its source, its purpose, its cause; although the phenomenon was clear enough, many years were to pass before I bothered to examine what was behind it: as with existentialism and doubtless many other observations, I failed to follow this 'political' aberration to its logical conclusion.

Which leaves me astonished now to think I was almost 30 before I peered beyond my own comfortable techno-bubble to recognise how corrupt cultures were anywhere in the world and how decrepit Western society in particular was for the majority of 'enslaved' people as elucidated in Laing's brilliant *'Politics of Experience'*

16

Sleep

EXERCISE AND FOOD have been examined almost to exhaustion in recent years with regard to feeling good, being healthy etc. Everyone surely knows about junk food and how it negatively affects health and mood, even if it elevates mood temporarily most junk food has negative long-tern effects. Likewise exercise: we all know that regular exercise keeps us healthy and, crucially, feeling good - both brain and body, like a single organism.

Sleep, on the other hand, is for some not so easy to control. The following represents my understanding of the issue from what I've experienced, read and heard on radio.

Apparently, a third of the population suffer from sleep problems. It seems that the most probable cause of insomnia - difficulty getting to SLEEP or not sleeping long enough - is anxiety or an overactive brain, too active for the restful state necessary for sleep.

And it's possible that Gwynith Lewis's observation in the final paragraph of the preceding chapter, which is about curing depression, could equally apply to insomnia: *the consequences of refusing to accept truth.*

Sometimes our subconscious mind knows something that our conscious mind, unaware of the subconscious, refuses to accept. This presents a dilemma, a conflict. We may have no idea of what is causing our mind's restless state. So if we re-examine carefully issues near the front of our thoughts, concerns and problems that we have failed to think over properly in the light of everything – then we might discover what our subconscious has observed that our conscious has been too preoccupied or proud, whatever, to notice.

Denial of facts we don't like can be responsible for a multitude of psychological problems, and can create internal conflicts that only grow. Attempting, for instance, to maintain a belief in God or some other supernatural entity *after* having awakened to the self-evident rationale that it's a myth, is, apparently, a common cause of internal conflict. Observe the dozens of cults and religions that continue to flourish. Do we really need these kinds of synthetic support? Maybe some of us do, at least temporarily, though like alcohol or cannabis it can have disturbing side effects.

Although I'd never seen nor heard of what I call 'star-meditation', it seems to me such an obvious technique that I'd be surprised if it hasn't been around for several millennia. It may be applicable for trying to get to sleep by focusing the mind away from intrusive persistent ruminating that sticks like an earworm. Here's an excerpt from my story *'Revealing Traits'* where the previously gloomy protagonist, Yop, attends a private consultation with a Guru:

> *'Be who you are,'* says the Guru, *'Submit to the silent mind. And your future will bear fruit as only a child can conceive.'*
>
> Again that infectious grin which Yop returns amplified. Now, though, she is entirely composed and rested. *'Thank you.'* she says, *'I feel much better already. You have helped me a lot. But you don't seem like a Guru. I was expecting, well, a sort of sombre, holy man. Whereas you are so cheerful and funny.'*
>
> *'Expectations, appearances... Poof!'* exclaims the Guru loudly, smiling so broadly his teeth resemble notes on a piano, *'Take the moment for what it offers, expect little and you will never know disappointments, of which I discern you have experienced many.'*
>
> *'How can you tell?'* she asks.

'Balance.' replies the Guru, now in a joyful high-pitched voice, as though his answer is simplistically obvious, 'Everything must be in balance. It always shows so clearly. Only when we strive to be other than what we truly are do we create imbalance.'

Now they sit calmly, and a few moments later the Guru resumes, his voice tranquil and soft, 'Lay back in the cushion now and relax, especially your neck and shoulders.'

Yop willingly obliges.

'Close your eyes.' he goes on very slowly, pausing between sentences, 'Imagine a sky of stars... Pick two and look between them for a fainter, more distant star... Look beyond that further into the emptiness, searching for a fainter star... Now look deeper still, for a yet fainter one... Rest your attention now as you direct your sight beyond it. You are looking hard into the infinite black void, trying to see deeper and deeper beyond the furthest, faintest star... Look ever deeper, into the great backdrop of empty black space which is your mind at peace.'

Unable to help herself, Yop effortlessly follows the Guru's directions. All is silent now, even the quiet sitar music ceases to play in her mind.

After what seems to Yop like a minute, but which is actually closer to ten, the Guru speaks again: 'Now you are tracing back from the void, the stars recede past you and your mind is returning, leaving its confusions to dissolve harmlessly in those furthest reaches of outer-space.' And after another delay he adds, 'Now open your eyes.'

Completely refreshed, Yop looks at him, at the mysterious homely twinkle in his eyes, and sits up again.

'Always remember your great wealth,' begins the Guru again shortly, 'And spend it generously, for the more you spend the more you will accumulate... I see your past through the years. You have been fortunate. Your recent troubles represent but a veneer of dust, much of which has now fallen away. What remains will soon follow. It is quite clear that you have now emerged from your cocoon.'

As to my own circumstances regarding sleep: Being an inveterate idler has several key advantages: for one thing, I simply refuse to be sufficiently concerned about anything to suffer preoccupation to the extent that it interferes with sleep. And for another, since I'm inclined to avoid effort at any opportunity, so my life is virtually free from obligations or stress.

There's always a few exceptions, but generally I just don't take anything seriously enough to fret about, even if it's me in control. Besides, anything can be better dwelt on tomorrow, I tell myself, when I'll be more awake. Plus, there's that little phenomenon about problems getting sorted in your subconscious while you sleep, so you wake up and, as if a light has come on in your head, like magic the solution appears: Eureka!

Hence, it's unusual if I have trouble getting to sleep. I usually read as soon as I'm in bed but rarely get through more than a couple of pages before drifting off. Of the times when sleep has eluded me, it hasn't done so for long – I just imagine myself preparing to head out towards the asteroids in a flying saucer that has unlimited capabilities. So far, I don't think I've ever got beyond Earth orbit.

If I'm not really tired, I'll simply get up and read or watch telly - what's the point in fighting wakefulness when you can actually take advantage? If you have to get up for work the next day, you can be sure that your body-clock will keep you awake for it but then you'll be tired sooner the following night and get a much better kip. And for me, since also (luckily) my financial circumstances - though not particularly lucrative - are stable, I have no reason to dwell on material issues; which could be another common source of preoccupation to avoid.

If I can be said to have a sleep problem then it would be that I sleep too much - frequently more than 8-hours - and it's with some regret that I almost never witness that amazing effect from getting out, especially in summer, to experience the scents and sensations that only happen (and are so powerfully felt) at dawn. I haven't heard the morning-chorus for years - and when I have heard it - as a youth many years ago - it's been when returning very late from a night out, and probably still half-drunk!

Which reminds me: I've also read that frequent early waking, while still tired, can be due to depression - these things interrelate - though I guess it might also be due to anxiety about getting up in time to go to dreaded work!

There's also the fact that the brain *needs* to sleep in order to assimilate the day's events. If the day has been uneventful, then the brain won't be so in need of sleep. Here's the final paragraph of my insane story *'The Speed Capsule'* (also a fine escape story for diving into soporific adventures).

> ....*'I reckon it's been a pretty sensational day.' observed Dippy, 'And Mad Zoot is a pretty amazing guy.'*
>
> *'I agree.' said Sop, as they approached where they would split three ways to go to their respective homes, 'And I reckon I've learned more today than in a whole year at school.'*
>
> *'Yeah.' added Piffle, as they separated, 'Me too. See you lot at the pier around 09.30 tomorrow, OK? And bring some dough.'*
>
> *They all waved.*
>
> *That night - and for the next three nights - they slept extremely soundly, for it is well known that any new experience is a highly effective soporific. And they'd had more new experience that day than most of us get in a decade.*
>
> *Goodnight.....*

I have to say, though, that there's hardly a day when I fail to engage in active brain-work. Just a walk, a bit of reading or writing, or listening to a good radio play, involves considerable brain-work – unconscious brain work mostly, it doesn't have to be anything taxing. Somehow, though, watching TV presents the brain with scarcely any effort. I guess the director and camera-man have done the work your brain would for a radio play or a book. So too much banal non-activity like watching TV, which somehow fails to stimulate the appropriate parts of the brain, is probably best avoided or minimised, or at least supplemented.

Another key detail to remember - AND THEN FORGET - is that like good sex, yawning, and even sneezing (and maybe several other things too) thinking about them can spoil the spontaneous natural process. This definitely goes for many aspects of life - reflecting on whether you're feeling happy, say - but when it comes to body functions I think it's more true than ever: it allows subconscious freedom from one's conscious controlling mind which usually has little idea about how to handle the body.

If the conscious mind wasn't so determined to dominate everything, then I think we'd all be a lot better off. So try listening more to your subconscious - by stilling the conscious to silence (which is what Zen is meant to do - and can be called-up at any time, just before sex might be good).

* * * * *

All this means that to tackle sleep problems, it's worth first examining and eliminating those causal factors: insufficient new experiences (ie, brain-work), anxiety, preoccupation and depression.

If you get on an aeroplane: once you're in, there's no sense in dwelling on the possibility of a crash - the issue is out of your hands. Why not try a similar approach when you get into bed?

Most people in the UK, so far as I can gather, are not nearly so concerned or irritated as I am about the elitism of government (ie, the way they subsidise wealth, while refusing a fair income for the poor). Nor, above all, do most people seem agitated, like me, by the blatant State terror, genocide and plunder the UK government together with other Western countries continually commit around the world. By far the majority of victims are civilians - mostly women, kids and helpless old folk - yet somehow none of this causes me any loss of sleep.

I rationalise that this is principally because it's beyond my control. It could also be because the issue preoccupies my left 'intellectual' brain and not my right 'emotional' brain - which I suppose is due to my lack of proximity or direct participation (ie, not knowing anyone involved). In other words: *essentially* I'm detached from the horror. However many emails I send to the local MP, or whatever else I do about it, my influence is nil. I am powerless. And I think this is a crucial point.

It implies that we are unlikely to have trouble sleeping when our conscience is clear - that is, when we have no pressing obligation that we've failed to meet. So another possible cause of insomnia could be our failure to address some issue that we should *and could* have addressed - and our subconscious refuses to leave us in peace till we've addressed it. Perhaps this is the most common cause of insomnia - caused by taking on too many obligations. The solution is obvious: sort your responsibilities then become an idler like me and avoid all but what's most essential.

A couple of decades ago I looked after my mum for several years. And it's true that no-one could have been easier or more of a pleasure to look after. But because I took on no other obligation, I didn't need to idle so far as she was concerned, yet I still managed to have loads of idling time.... the little Zen story *'Is That So?'* comes to mind.

Now for a good kip...

.. ....zzzzzzzzzzzzZZZZ

.
.
.
.

17

Hell is Other People

ESSENTIALLY, THAT'S THE THEME of this book (as stated by Sartre and demonstrated in his play 'No Exit'). When I was a kid I was baffled why adults were so often inclined to treat me with disrespect and disregard. Why was I made to feel contingent? Why was I so frequently ignored or disparaged? Why was it me who had to sit on the floor if there weren't enough chairs? Why was I not allowed to make or contribute to decisions and choices? Why was it me who was always wrong, did things badly, was generally considered a pest, made to feel unwanted?

I say all this and yet I was one of the lucky few, I now realise. The above applies to me only partially; mostly these anomalies were experienced at school and elsewhere, not at home. Philip Larkin's famous poem doesn't apply to me, as it does to many people:

> *They fuck you up, your mum and dad.*
> *They may not mean to, but they do.*
> *They fill you with the faults they had*
> *And add some extra, just for you.*
>
> *But they were fucked up in their turn*
> *By fools in old-style hats and coats,*
> *Who half the time were soppy-stern*
> *And half at one another's throats.*
>
> *Man hands on misery to man.*
> *It deepens like a coastal shelf.*

Get out as early as you can,
And don't have any kids yourself.

Alas, Larkin's great poem is all to often appropriate. Too many of us as adults lack the insight to how our behaviour affects kids in our charge - how some seemingly trivial decision by us can have a devastating impact on a kid's sense of self and sense of autonomy. Too often we fail to recognise how crucial this sense of self is, and of the shattering consequences for the individual who is denied its natural development.

Being dominated, feeling powerless etc., are profound sensations. When imposed over a long period or repeated over and over at an early age, no amount of therapy later can reverse the effect or compensate so the victim will fully recover. Such cruelty, whether deliberate or not, has a terrible and lasting impact. Many lives have been destroyed in this way, when all that's needed to avoid it is a moment of poise, of rational reflection. Just small efforts of consideration can make all the difference.

How do you feel when someone ignores you or frequently contradicts you or dominates you? How do you feel when someone repeatedly breaks an agreement or promise? If it's just one person, even if someone close, you might get by fine. But supposing everyone acts in this way towards you, then what? Maybe we just need one person we can trust totally and can rely on? A kid especially, I think, can survive psychologically if they have one person at least they can rely on for full support.

These issues should be seen as of paramount importance for us all, mostly for kids, but all of us surely should treat one another with respect and fairness and kindness. The world seems to have become a monumental rip-off, outfits maximising profits at the expense of the poorest who they don't give a rap for. Society these days has become a battleground with everyone fighting 'tooth-&-nail' to survive.

Have you seen *'The Little Book of Calm'*? I have, in the bookshop, but I didn't need to even open it. I can guess what's in it - or some of what's in it. I wonder if it tells us that reading how to live calmly achieves nothing unless we practice it?

So we need to practice, and we need reminders.... As I've described, Pyotr Ouspensky's reminder for 'self-remembering' (as he referred to bringing himself into the NOW) was *'the lamppost trick'* – when he saw a lamppost he'd immediately think: "NOW" and ditch anything else he was thinking about that was past or future, and focus on what he was doing at that moment, feeling the pavement on the soles of his feet, the air on his face, the tenseness in his shoulders, the beauty of clouds in the sky right this instant...

When we address a kid on an issue, or anyone for that matter, find some reminder like Ouspensky's lamppost that will bring you alert to the moment so you don't just brush the kid aside, but give them time, give all your attention – don't they deserve it? But not just the kid... anyone... or, for that matter, anything you happen to be doing.

I have to say, I'm a terrible hypocrite here. I fail constantly at all these things, and I've been working at grasping 'the-NOW' for decades. So practice.... I tell myself.

A couple of decades ago I spent about 15-months working part-time as a BT telephone operator. The operator centre comprised a huge room with more than 100 operators. Every now and then you'd hear a gasp and a loud click when an annoyed operator had received a disgruntled or abusive call. Since we were all completely anonymous to a caller, why would anyone take personally what a caller might say? The idea strikes me as ludicrous. So how can I be offended or even annoyed? My response to such callers was, as a kind-of challenge, to convert them from an angry, unhappy frame of mind to precisely the opposite. I'd respond in the most appropriately polite and sympathetic way I could to even the worst language and abusive outburst. I'd offer refunds, free calls (both of which were permitted) and discuss as pleasantly, and affably as possible, always courteous and making sure to avoid sounding condescending or flippant. Generally it worked well and left me feeling as though I'd really achieved something to leave the customer (or trickster, who cares?) contented. To bring light to someone gloomy or angry is a worthwhile thing to do, I reckon. I'd also, to the supervisor's annoyance - you can't avoid annoying someone just a little now and then - encourage mischievous kids in public call boxes in those pre-mobile phone days. Always create a bit of fun whenever possible, never mind officialdom, is my angle.

The following could be from any good psychology book because it should be general knowledge, and probably is for psychologists. I've copied it from 'A Therapeutic Journey' by Alain de Botton:

WHAT A BAD PARENT CAN DO TO A CHILD

The power of a bad parent is almost without limit. Within only a few years, a bad parent might be able to create an offspring who:

is convinced that they are unworthy hates themselves without limit

is perpetually certain that they have done something very wrong

constantly anticipates catastrophe

loathes their own appearance

fears everyone's rage and envy

cannot enjoy sex

is unable to explore their mind

always feels they need to agree, comply and people-please

can't show their true self for fear of revolting everyone

will never put a stop to their own abuse, in whatever form this comes

has to puff themselves up with money and acclaim to feel acceptable

is compelled to torture others as they were tortured

cannot tolerate ambiguity and criticism

cannot play

must always be right

has to sabotage anything promising, kind and good that enters their life

And that's just to start the list.

18

Conclusion

This book seems to have become like a golf course with 18 holes where this chapter is the last, your final drive at the freeway. Which clubs or irons have you used? Did you score more birdies or more bogies.... or even a few eagles, maybe an ace - a hole in one? How did you perform in the first 17? I guess a par would be to complete a chapter feeling you enjoyed reading it and understood its point and significance, that it made sense but maybe needs a re-read or more time to sink in? Supposing I wrote so lucidly that every chapter was an ACE, wouldn't that be something?

I've never played real golf, and maybe it's a crazy metaphor? However, there are some real masters of psychology and highly articulate instruction out there. On youtube you can find many great lectures from people like:

Ajahn Brahm - BUDDHIST SOCIETY OF WESTERN AUSTRALIA

Alan Watts

R D Laing

... and doubtless others.

Those are just the three I most recommend and have dipped into now and then over several years. There must be many like them I haven't seen, possible even better than they are. But for all their genius and edifying talk, for all their skills of eloquence and entertainment, the key is always to practice....

as I say, you can watch a hundred brilliant lessons on how to play a guitar from Joscho Stephan, say, but unless you practice on your own guitar - on your own mind - then it's all mere entertainment, which is fine.... nothing wrong with being entertained... but like the ocean I describe in chapte-9, you only see the surface, when the real essence is to be found in the vastness beneath - that's to say: in the practice. To penetrate and liberate the subconscious: practice. The subconscious is, I believe, like nine-tenths of the iceberg of mind below the conscious surface. After a slow start comes a glimmer of hope, then the slight sense of achievement, and soon the joy in moving above and away from the proverbial abyss you skirted for so long, so long...

Appendix

Trees

by Hermann Hesse

For me, trees have always been the most penetrating preachers. I revere them when they live in tribes and families, in forests and groves. And even more I revere them when they stand alone. They are like lonely persons. Not like hermits who have stolen away out of some weakness, but like great, solitary men, like Beethoven and Nietzsche. In their highest boughs the world rustles, their roots rest in infinity; but they do not lose themselves there, they struggle with all the force of their lives for one thing only: to fulfil themselves according to their own laws, to build up their own form, to represent themselves. Nothing is holier, nothing is more exemplary than a beautiful, strong tree. When a tree is cut down and reveals its naked death-wound to the sun, one can read its whole history in the luminous, inscribed disc of its trunk: in the rings of its years, its scars, all the struggle, all the suffering, all the sickness, all the happiness and prosperity stand truly written, the narrow years and the luxurious years, the attacks withstood, the storms endured. And every young farm-boy knows that the hardest and noblest wood has the narrowest rings, that high on the mountains and in continuing danger the most indestructible, the strongest, the ideal trees grow.

Trees are sanctuaries. Whoever knows how to speak to them, whoever knows how to listen to them, can learn the truth. They do not preach learning and precepts, they preach, undeterred by particulars, the ancient law of life.

The tree says: A kernel is hidden with in me, a spark, a thought, I am life from eternal life. The attempt and the risk that the eternal mother took with me is unique, unique the form and veins of my skin, unique the smallest play of leaves in my branches and the smallest scar on my bark. I was made to form and reveal the eternal in my smallest special detail.

A tree says: my strength is trust. I know nothing about my fathers, I know nothing about the thousand children that every year spring out of me. I live out the secret of my seed to the very end, and I care for nothing else. I trust that God is in me. I trust that my labour is holy. Out of this trust I live.

When we are stricken and cannot bear our lives any longer, then a tree has something to say to us: Be still! Be still! Look at me! Life is not easy, life is not difficult. Those are childish thoughts. Let God speak within you, and your thoughts will grow silent. You are anxious because your path leads away from mother and home. But every step and every day lead you back again to the mother. Home is neither here nor there. Home is within you, or home is nowhere at all.

A longing to wander tears my heart when I hear trees rustling in the wind at evening. If one listens to them silently for a long time, this longing reveals its kernel, its meaning. It is not so much a matter of escaping from one's suffering, though it may seem to be so. It is a longing for home, for a memory of the mother, for new metaphors for life. It leads home. Every path leads homeward, every step is birth, every step is death, every grave is mother.

So the tree rustles in the evening, when we stand uneasy before our own childish thought. Trees have long thoughts, long-breathing and restful, just as they have longer lives than ours. There are wiser than we are, as long as we do not listen to them. But when we have learned how to listen to trees, then the brevity and quickness and the childlike hastiness of our thoughts achieve an incomparable joy. Whoever has learned how to listen to trees no longer wants to be a tree. He wants to be nothing except what he is. That is home. That is happiness.

Printed in Great Britain
by Amazon

34530522R00057